INSIGHT ⊙ GUIDES

EXPLORE

WASHINGTON, DC

⊙ Walking Eye App

YOUR FREE EBOOK AVAILABLE THROUGH THE WALKING EYE APP

Your guide now includes a free eBook to your chosen destination, for the same great price as before. Simply download the Walking Eye App from the App Store or Google Play to access your free eBook.

HOW THE WALKING EYE APP WORKS

Through the Walking Eye App, you can purchase a range of eBooks and destination content. However, when you buy this book, you can download the corresponding eBook for free. Just see below in the grey panel where to find your free content and then scan the QR code at the bottom of this page.

Destinations: Download essential destination content featuring recommended sights and attractions, restaurants, hotels and an A–Z of practical information, all available for purchase.

Ships: Interested in ship reviews? Find independent reviews of river and ocean ships in this section, all available for purchase.

eBooks: You can download your free accompanying digital version of this guide here. You will also find a whole range of other eBooks, all available for purchase.

Free access to travel-related blog articles about different destinations, updated on a daily basis.

HOW THE EBOOKS WORK

The eBooks are provided in EPUB file format. Please note that you will need an eBook reader installed on your device to open the file. Many devices come with this as standard, but you may still need to install one manually from Google Play.

The eBook content is identical to the content in the printed guide.

HOW TO DOWNLOAD THE WALKING EYE APP

1. Download the Walking Eye App from the App Store or Google Play.
2. Open the app and select the scanning function from the main menu.
3. Scan the QR code on this page – you will then be asked a security question to verify ownership of the book.
4. Once this has been verified, you will see your eBook in the purchased ebook section, where you will be able to download it.

Other destination apps and eBooks are available for purchase separately or are free with the purchase of the Insight Guide book.

CONTENTS

ACCESSIBILITY

Smithsonian museums offer audio, tactile, and ASL tours. The National Archives has copies of the Constitution and Declaration of Independence in Braille and services for deaf visitors (routes 5 and 6).

RECOMMENDED ROUTES FOR...

ARCHITECTURAL INTEREST

Take tours that highlight the beauty and symbolism of the Capitol, Library of Congress (route 2), and National Building Museum (route 9). Stroll through the restored Union Station (route 9).

ART MUSEUMS

The National Gallery of Art holds collections by the Masters (route 6), while the National Museum of Women in the Arts showcases female artists (route 10). Dumbarton Oaks has an incredible Byzantine and pre-Columbian collection (route 8).

FAMILIES

After you finish at the Smithsonian museums on the Mall (routes 5 and 6), watch money being printed at the National Bureau of Engraving and Printing (route 4). Discover secret doors at the Mansion on O Street (route 11) or spend a day with the animals at the National Zoo (route 11).

GARDENS

Don't miss Bartholdi Park and the US Botanic Garden (route 2). Dumbarton Oaks is a 10-acre oasis of terraced landscapes and fountains (route 8).

HISTORY BUFFS

The three major documents of American Democracy are at the National Archives (route 6). Relive the events surrounding Lincoln's Assassination at Ford's Theatre (route 10). Review American pre-industrial life at the Daughters of the American Revolution Museum (route 7).

LITERARY TYPES

See a Shakespeare First Folio at the Folger Shakespeare Library and exhibits from the overwhelming collections at the Library of Congress (route 2). Browse until the small hours at Kramerbooks and the Afterwords Café (route 12).

SHOPPING

Union Station has upscale and specialty shops in the beautifully restored travel terminal (route 9). M Street NW and Wisconsin Avenue are shopping hubs in Georgetown (route 8). DuPont Circle is known for art galleries and specialty shops (route 12).

INTRODUCTION

An introduction to Washington, DC's geography, customs, and culture, plus illuminating background information on cuisine, history, and what to do when you're there.

The Lincoln Memorial

EXPLORE WASHINGTON, DC

Originally a quiet town that was merely a footnote to world politics, Washington, DC is now arguably the center of global and national power and a magnet for world culture, education, arts, and entertainment.

Washington was created with one purpose – as the seat of government for the fledgling United States of America. It was designed to reflect the dignity and importance of its mission with broad boulevards and grand vistas, stately buildings, and impressive monuments – all of this at a time when the country was viewed with curiosity and amusement, more than respect, by European powers.

Its ambiance is the pursuit of power by elected officials, lobbyists, activists, policy wonks, pundits, analysts, and consultants. But it is also a city that, in many other ways, reflects the country it represents. The problems of economic and racial inequality, urban poverty and neglect, crime, education, and infrastructure mar the psyche of much of the city's population. Because it is the focus of so much national and international attention, the ways in which DC addresses those problems are closely watched by the rest of the country and the world.

As the center of the military-industrial-political world, it was targeted in the 9-11 terrorist attack and the security measures enforced throughout

the city are constant reminders that DC is still an attractive mark. Meanwhile, the temper of the government since the 2017 inauguration of President Donald Trump means a constant, chaotic display of democracy, with demonstrations, protests, and political action.

GEOGRAPHY AND LAYOUT

Washington's location is the result of a compromise between northern and southern politicians. In exchange for wiping out the north's Revolutionary War debt, they agreed to allow the capital to be built in the south, but not too far south. The Potomac River border between Maryland and Virginia was 'southern' but comfortably close to Philadelphia and New York.

Major Pierre L'Enfant was handpicked by George Washington to plan the 'Federal City.' (Washington objected to the place being named after him.) L'Enfant's designed a diamond-shaped grid, bisected by two Capitol Streets: Capitol North-South and Capitol East-West. Streets running north–south are numbered;

Cobblestone street in Georgetown

those running east–west are lettered. In addition, there are streets running diagonally across the city, which are named after states. Streets have a suffix to indicate in which quadrant of the city it lays. A typical address might be 1417 A Avenue SW or 332 12th Street NE.

Washington is best experienced on foot. Most points of interest are relatively close to each other. Each tour in this book focuses on a specific area, featuring its most visited or important sites and some lesser-known, but valuable, attractions. However, there is a lot of territory to cover, so wear comfortable shoes.

Public transportation is well planned and affordable. The DC Circulator bus has several interconnected routes that travel through the most popular tourist areas. Taxis are everywhere, but much more expensive. Uber is also popular. The Metro subway system is easy to navigate and is most useful for traveling between downtown and outlying areas.

HISTORY

Until World War II, Washington was still a modest city, but with the US entry into the war, the Federal Government expanded exponentially. In the decades since, the bureaucracy has continued to grow, along with think tanks, consultants, business and civic organizations, and lobbyists.

The city is a magnet for demonstrations. From the massive Civil Rights-era March on Washington in 1963, through protests of the Vietnam War, anti-Wall Street Occupy Washington tent city, and the Women's March and March for Science in 2017, to smaller displays outside embassies, and on street corners, the capital draws thousands who display their concerns. Expect to see someone demonstrating for or against something somewhere during your travels.

CLIMATE

Washington's summers are summed up by the '3 H's' – hazy, hot, and humid. In July and August, it's common for both the temperature and humidity

A summer's evening in Adams Morgan

Washington Harbour

to be in the 90s (30°C and 90 percent humidity). Afternoon thunderstorms are common.

The warm weather begins in May and continues through late September. The spring and fall are delightful, with comfortable daytime highs, cool nights, and clear skies.

Winter is unpredictable. Expect it to be cold and damp. Most years see very little snowfall, although the years between 2010–16 saw several record-breaking blizzards. Generally, temperatures hover around freezing (32°F/0°C), but expect a week or more in January and February when the mercury drops into single digits (5°F/-15°C).

The best time to visit is in April–May and mid-September–October when not only is the weather better, there are fewer tourists.

POPULATION

The city of Washington occupies 61 sq miles (158 sq km) on the Potomac and Anacostia rivers and bordering Maryland and Virginia.

The population of the city was 681,000 in 2016. Including the suburbs that figure grows to over 6 million. The northwest quadrant is the largest and most affluent area. About 50 percent of the population are African Americans residing primarily in the northeast, southeast, and southwest quadrants. While many of those areas are still mired in poverty, others,

like Logan Circle (see page 76), are developing as trendy neighborhoods.

Much of the interest stems from the lower-priced houses and apartments in those areas. The average monthly rent for a one-bedroom apartment in Washington is $2,000 and the median price for a house is $550,000. With a median age of 34 and a median per capita income of $50,000, young professionals view moving into a less-developed neighborhood as economic survival and a good investment.

Increased development of shopping malls and entertainment areas in the southwest and southeast along the waterfront has seen a lot of low-income housing being sold by landlords for redevelopment. The question of where these former residents go is still unanswered.

About 44 percent of the population is white, and 4 percent is Hispanic. As befits an international metropolis, many other nationalities are represented, although in small groups. The Adams Morgan neighborhood (see page 106) northeast of DuPont Circle is home to many immigrant groups, giving the neighborhood a lively diversity.

LOCAL CUSTOMS

Washington buzzes with a sense of purpose. There's great energy surrounding Capitol Hill where legislation is argued, the headquarters of gov-

The NMAAHC building

Dining in the city's hip Shaw neighborhood

ernment agencies where policies are crafted and administered, the museums and monuments where visitors experience art and history, and the neighborhoods where residents work and play.

The city wakes very early, but visitors can wait until after the morning rush hour to begin touring. Most museums are open 10am–5pm, with some staying open later.

During the day, the pace downtown is busy, but as soon as offices and museums close, the streets are deserted. DC's nightlife is in DuPont Circle, Logan Circle, Georgetown, Capitol Hill South, and along the developing Southwest Waterfront

DON'T LEAVE WASHINGTON, DC WITHOUT...

Viewing DC from the Post Office Tower. This is the best choice for seeing DC from above; on a clear day, you'll also see the Blue Ridge Mountains. See page 74.

Rising early to see the pandas. The National Zoo grounds open at 6am in the summer, 8am in the winter. Get there as early as possible as Pandas are most active in the mornings. See page 82.

Enjoying the New Vegas Lounge. This Logan Circle landmark is the go-to place for live Rhythm and Blues on weekends. The 'Out of Town Blues Band' has worked with every major name in the genre. See page 106.

Spotting Darth Vader on the National Cathedral. During renovations, schoolchildren suggested adding the Star Wars villain as a new gargoyle. You will need binoculars to find him near the top of the northwest tower. See page 81.

Finding nature on Roosevelt Island. Trails meander through this memorial to the outdoorsman in the Potomac. Metrorail serves the island, but a more active way to reach it is to rent a kayak

from Thompson Boat Center and paddle across. See page 25.

Crossing the 'Barnes Dance'. Named for the traffic engineer who designed it, this pedestrian crossing by the Friendship Arch is decorated with colorful symbols of the Chinese Zodiac. See page 70.

Strolling through Obama's neighborhood. The exclusive Kalorama neighborhood became high profile when both former President Obama and Ivanka Trump moved in. You won't get close to Obama's home, but Ivanka's is not obviously guarded. See page 79.

Buying lunch from a food truck. The mobile kitchens line the streets every day at lunchtime. Every cuisine is on offer, as are desserts and other treats. See page 108.

Sitting in Einstein's lap. The Einstein Memorial behind the National Academy of Sciences is a huge statue of him lounging with a sheaf of papers in his hand. It's impossible to resist climbing onto the scientist's lap and posing for a photo. See page 63.

(see page 38). Restaurants and clubs are busy, but this is a working town. Late nights are not the norm. By midnight, most people are tucked up in bed. On weekends, people catch up on mundane errands, shopping, or seeking out relaxing activities: visiting Eastern Farmers' Market, Rock Creek Park, attending festivals or concerts, or viewing exhibits they don't have time to visit during the week.

POLITICS AND ECONOMICS

Washington is in the odd position of being a city that has a government but is not allowed to fully govern itself. It has a Mayor – currently Muriel Bowser – and 13-member City Council. The Mayor enforces city laws, and has the power to sign or veto bills passed by the Council. She oversees all city services, public agencies, police and fire departments, and the public schools.

However, her actions and the decisions of the City Council are ultimately controlled by Congress, which retains the right to intervene in local affairs. This was established in the Constitution and the District of Columbia Home Rule Act in 1973. The district has a non-voting delegate to the House of Representatives, who may sit on committees, participate in debates, and even introduce legislation. Unlike other US territories – like Puerto Rico or Guam, which also have non-voting delegates – residents of DC must pay federal taxes.

Referendums have repeatedly shown that the residents want statehood (in 2016, the vote was 86 percent in favor of statehood), but proposals have been blocked by Congress. Opponents claim that statehood would destroy the idea of a separate, independent capital and would unfairly grant representation to a single city. Republicans fear that the mostly Democratic population of Washington would elect Democratic senators and representatives, giving that party an advantage. There are also concerns about following laws that affect the ability of federal security forces allowed to operate in a state. As a pointed reminder from citizens of their frustration and of the impetus for the American Revolution, the city's unofficial motto, 'Taxation Without Representation' is on DC license plates.

Washington is somewhat protected against economic swings because the money that flows from lobbyists, associations, and government activities is a few steps removed from the general economy. The periodic government shutdowns stemming from one-upmanship games in Congress have negative effects but are usually temporary or impact individuals and specific venues, rather than causing long-term damage to the city as a whole.

The Mama Ayesha's Restaurant Mural depicting US presidents from Eisenhower to Obama

Overall, Washington, DC is the hub of history, current affairs, and culture. It's a place that never stagnates and where something fresh, interesting, inspiring, and stimulating is always happening. It's a city filled with monuments to the past where the people and visitors of the present keep the history alive and exciting.

TOP TIPS FOR VISITING WASHINGTON, DC

Mind the weather. Summers in Washington are brutal. Try to stay indoors mid-day. When walking, pace yourself, stay hydrated, and wear a hat. The rest of the year, wear layers. Even on chilly days, you will warm up when walking.

Plan off-peak visits. Attractions are often less busy mid-week and late afternoon. Try visiting an hour before closing. The monuments along the Reflecting Pool and Tidal Basin never close. Visit at night or in the early morning for quiet contemplation.

Get tickets for attractions if needed. A few museums require pre-reserved, timed tickets (see websites for details). The Museum of African American History and Culture requires them year-round. The Holocaust Memorial Museum requires them March through August. Reserve online as far in advance as possible. Some special exhibits also require tickets.

Discount and free tickets. Visit www.goldstar.com/washington-dc for deals on shows and activities across the city; www.dctheatrescene.com specializes in discount theater tickets.

Police and security. Washington is protected by the DC Metropolitan Police, Secret Service, US Capitol Police, Supreme Court Police, National Park Service Police, US Marshalls, and others. They are almost always unfailingly polite, and many know the city as well as tour guides. But their first job is to provide security. Follow their instructions and treat them with respect and courtesy.

Crossing signals. There are pedestrian crossing signals and crosswalks at many intersections. Drivers are generally very good about respecting them. Don't cross on a red light or in the middle of the block.

Numbering building floors. The ground level\street level floor is considered the 1st floor. The level immediately above that is the 2nd floor.

Trash cans. Common elsewhere, they are rare near the White House, Capitol, and government buildings. Carry garbage until you can discard of it properly.

Take in the full experience. Nothing in DC is without symbolism. Observe the buildings and appreciate the detail on them. Always view the orientation films. They give background and context that will enhance your visit.

Visiting with your dog. Many hotels welcome dogs, but check the website and ask for details when making reservations. Dogs are not allowed in buildings or in the sculpture gardens along the Mall. Clean up after your pet. Many restaurants allow dogs if there is outdoor seating.

Fresh lobster at the Maine Avenue Fish Market

FOOD AND DRINK

With trendsetting chefs, international cuisines, and hugely popular local spots, Washington's dining scene is as diverse as its politics. Add in a lively bar culture and DC becomes a foodie destination in its own right.

After decades of enduring a reputation as an epicurean's nightmare of mediocre steakhouses and overpriced highballs, Washington has evolved into an internationally appreciated dining and drink destination. Any lingering doubts about the transformation were erased when the esteemed Michelin Guide issued its first guide to Washington in 2016. The 2018 guide lists three two-star and eleven one-star restaurants.

There are more restaurants per capita in Washington than in New York City. More money is spent on dining here than in other major metropolitan areas. While much of that comes from tourists and expense account meals, most is spent by locals.

Much of this reflects the city's demographics. The average age of the population is in the mid-30s. They live in up-and-coming neighborhoods like Logan Circle and Capitol Hill South, and they view dining as a social activity and a form of entertainment. They are eager to try new culinary experiences and are quick to spread the word about interesting menus and venues.

For young chefs, it's an ideal climate to apply their skills in creating innovative and exciting menus. They are a tightly knit community who appreciate each other and who manage to simultaneously support, encourage, and compete.

LOCAL CUISINE

Michelin defines the local cuisine as 'Mid-Atlantic.' That reflects the availability and use of regional ingredients and traditional recipes. Immigrants from Europe brought their culinary traditions with them. Familiar dishes eased the longing for family and homes left behind. Slaves managed to recreate food ways taken from them by captivity and created new dishes with the unfamiliar ingredients they found on farms and plantations. As these groups intermingled, recipes and ingredients were shared and blended.

Chefs boast of local sourcing and farm-to-table approaches. The Chesapeake Bay with its bounty of seafood plays a major role. The region's fertile farmland supports a wide variety of crops and good grazing for livestock, and it's not uncommon for menus to list suppliers. Organic, chemical-free, grass-fed, free-range, and humanely raised are buzzwords seen often enough

Fully loaded burger at Woodward Table

that it's noticeable when they are missing. Most restaurants now highlight gluten-free options or warn customers if the kitchen cannot promise a gluten-free environment. The same is true of other allergens. Vegetarians can feel comfortable in DC. It is rare for a restaurant not to have vegetarian selections or to create a vegetarian entree if needed. Ask about children's menus. If there isn't one, chances are that the restaurant is not a good choice for a family meal.

WHERE TO EAT

It's easier to ask 'What are you in the mood for?' Washington is nothing if not accommodating for every taste, cuisine, mood, and budget. A meal at an exclusive restaurant can be a memorable highlight for a vacation. Stopping at a local gastropub lets your meet the locals in a casual setting. Many places have luncheon and happy hour (generally 4pm to 6 or 7pm) specials on meals and drinks, which helps stretch the budget.

High-end restaurants

Upscale restaurants are defined by price, of course, but there are other factors: the ambiance, the setting, the service, the location, and – ultimately – the food. Most of them are found near the center of downtown. DC's high-end listings cross a spectrum of discrete rooms with familiar entrees like Mastro's Steakhouse (see page 99) and Occidental Grill and Seafood (see page 99), exquisitely

prepared Italian and Spanish cuisine at Acqua Al 2 (see page 98) and Arroz (see page 99), and perfected homage to regional ingredients and traditions at Acadiana (see page 99).

International restaurants

With its international population of diplomats, immigrants, students, and visitors, Washington naturally has a huge number of ethnic restaurants, giving you a chance to experience the world one bite at a time. Wander up 18th Street in Adams Morgan and choose between Afghan, Japanese, and Middle Eastern restaurants. Many of the small storefronts are serving Grandma's recipes. In Logan Circle, Compass Rose (see page 103) serves street food from 30 countries, while DuPont Circle offers Mission (see page 101) for Mexican specialties and Zorba's Café (see page 101) for a trip to the Aegean.

Seafood

'The fish you eat today slept last night in the Chesapeake Bay.' So goes the slogan of one seafood-centric eatery. Imagining Washington without seafood on menus is like imagining Washington without politicians. Blue crab is the summer crustacean of choice. It will be on most menus, even at steak houses. Opt for broiled crab cakes and obscenely rich cream of crab soup, served with a dash of sherry. Oyster bars, serving varieties from the Chesapeake and elsewhere, are popular. Good options include Hank's Oyster Bar

Diners at Joselito Casa de Comidas

(see page 89), and Old Ebbitt Grill (see page 33).

Neighborhood pubs

It's the local places where the real Washington eats. If you want to talk to people other than tour guides and taxi drivers, seek out the cafés and explore streets a bit removed from the sightseeing spots and hotel row. The menus may not be the most innovative, but sometimes familiar and friendly is what vacations are all about. Capitol Hill South along Pennsylvania Avenue SE is dotted with neighborhood hangouts. Bullfeathers (see page 99) is the place for comfort food such as an honest burger. In Georgetown, Mr. Smith's of Georgetown (see page 102) has served regulars for 50 years and has as sing-along piano set.

Tasting menus

A nice way to explore a restaurant's offerings or to try a new cuisine is a tasting menu. For a set price you can get anywhere from 4 to 15 courses, often with paired drinks. Iron Gate (see page 102) is Mediterranean, Rasika (see page 98) is a wonderful introduction to Indian cuisine, and Joselito Casa de Comidas (see page 98) serves Spanish food from family recipes.

DRINKS

As with food, Washington's libation landscape is maturing. Mixologists routinely invent variations on standard cocktails like cosmos, martinis, and margaritas. But there's an undeclared war to see who can create the next 'gotta try it' cocktail. Often, that moves into the realm of near silliness with combinations that defy explanation, like nori seaweed and rum. Hot places come and go, but Hank's Cocktail Bar (819 Upshur Street NW; www.hankscocktailbar.com), Rosario (2435 18th Street NW; www.rosario.dc.com), and the Hemingway-inspired Bar Pilar (1833 14th Street NW; www.barpilar.com) are known for their new drinks. Give the bartender your choice of spirit and flavor at La Jambe (1550 7th Street NW; www.lajambedc.com) and he'll create a personal cocktail.

Beers

Craft beers are firmly in the mainstream, with bars able to choose from established breweries and offerings from the dozens of others that open each year. The first brewery to open in DC since Prohibition was Capitol City, in 1992. There are now at least ten. Look for 3 Stars, Right Proper, Gordon Biersch, and Bluejacket. Ask the bartender about

Whiskies at Jack Rose

Maine Avenue Fish Market

other local brews. Regional reliables are Dogfish Head, Heavy Seas, and Flying Dog. As with cocktails, brewers experiment with flavor combinations, like adding peppercorns or pecans. Want to try them all? Visit Churchkey (1337 14th Street NW; www.churchkey.com) with 50 drafts and a 30-page list of bottled beer.

Spirits

While not as advanced as the craft beer industry, Maryland and Virginia have several distilleries producing whiskies and ryes that owe much to the traditions of colonial distillers (like George Washington). You'll need to ask if the bar has local spirits, as most of them have a small distribution. One Eighth Distillery and New Columbia Distillery both sell small batch spirits at the DuPont Circle Farmer's Market (see box) on Sunday mornings. Ask for them at Jack Rose Dining Saloon, which serves 2,600 whiskies (2007 18th Street NW; www.jackrosediningsaloon.com).

Wines

Both Maryland and Virginia have highly respected wine industries, producing award-winning vintages from places as close as the Blue Ridge Mountains. Many restaurants, particularly those that emphasize local sourcing, have at least a few bottles of local wine on their wine list. If you want an international tasting experience, Cork Wine Bar (1805 14th Street NW; www.corkdc.com) pours 50 old-world wines by the glass.

Food markets

Washington's markets are theme parks of food. The oldest is the Eastern Market (225 7th Street NE; Eastern Market Metro station: Blue and Orange lines), founded in 1873. It is the anchor for the neighborhood, where shoppers connect with the vendors and each other. During the week, the great brick hall houses a dozen or so vendors selling fresh produce including seafood, deli meats, and fresh pastas. On Tuesdays, Saturdays, and Sundays farmers sell their fresh harvests and meats outside. Weekends see the market expand further still to include a high-end craft fair.

Union Market (1309 5th Street NE; NoMA-Gallaudet Metro stop: Red line) is a vast gourmet food hall with over 40 vendors in a modern, bright space. Between the specialty vendors selling spices, local sausages, and kombucha, and a vast kitchenware shop, the market feels like a culinary treasure house.

Voted one of the best outdoor farmers' markets in the country, the DuPont Circle Farmer's Market (1500 20th Street NW; DuPont Metro Stop: Red line) is open every Sunday morning, year-round. Joining the usual roster of fresh foods, vendors sell 'grandma's' baklava, fresh-made pastas, and Oriental dumplings. Right Proper beers, One Eighth Distillery, and New Columbia Distillery also sell beers, gin, vermouth, and artisanal liqueurs.

Bridge Street Books, Georgetown

SHOPPING

With malls selling exclusive designer goods, museum shops with unique gifts, and handicrafts offered in tiny storefronts, power politics has nothing over the power shopping in Washington. Great finds are waiting to be discovered throughout the city.

It used to be that shopping in Washington was confined to a few tired department stores, a scattering of specialty shops, and the souvenir trucks lining downtown streets. No more. Revitalization of neighborhoods and business districts and new developments along the waterfront has brought scores of new shops, many of which appeal to visitors.

WHAT TO LOOK FOR

Here you'll find exclusive designer fashions, well-known clothing labels, and boutiques introducing new designers, alongside vintage and new interior decorating accent pieces; antiques and collectibles; books; original and reproduction art; and handicrafts from around the world.

WHERE TO SHOP

Georgetown. This is easily the most eclectic and comprehensive neighborhood for finding whatever it is you desire, in addition to things you never thought you wanted. The intersection of M Street and Wisconsin Avenue is the heart of the shopping district. Most of the familiar clothing names and specialty national retailers are found along M Street. Hu's Wear and Hu's Shoes, Polo, and Alex and Ani fit you out in the latest styles and accessories, while Patagonia takes care of outdoor adventurers. Don't miss a wander up Wisconsin Avenue to find indie storefronts and boutiques introducing new designers and fashion accessories.

DuPont Circle. The other place for a great variety of shops, but less hectic and with an emphasis on independent stores. Brooks Brothers and Betsy Fisher are about the only 'names,' unless you count a branch of Lou Lou, the local chain of shops selling nice costume jewelry and accessories. Proper Topper sells hats, of course, but also other interesting accessories. Fashionistas gravitate to Secondi, the consignment outlet known for an outstanding selection of high-end designer clothing. The beloved Kramerbooks and Afterwords Café (see page 87) is a DC landmark, open until the small hours. Tabletop sells imaginative, useful, and suitcase-friendly homeware, knickknacks, and gifts.

City Center. This sparkling new development located in Chinatown aims to

Union Station store　　　　　　　　　*Phillips Collection museum shop*

become a 5th Avenue\Rodeo Drive-style residential and retail landmark. The broad breezeways connect the big names of haute couture: Hermès, Kate Spade, Gucci, and others. More modest national retail names – like Bed Bath & Beyond, Urban Outfitters, and Loft – are in the adjacent Gallery Place. As per city regulations, the names are shown in Chinese, as well as English.

U Street\14th Street Corridor. This is another area experiencing a transformation, but the vibe here is funky and fun, attracting young professionals. This is a good place to look for men's fashions, which seem to be overlooked in other areas. It also has an unusual number of stores selling home decor. And if vintage and secondhand shopping is your weakness, this is the place to come. Frank & Oak sell a good variety of men's clothes, Salt & Sundry has hip houseware and accent pieces, while ShInola sells quality leather goods.

Union Station. The station is worth a visit just to enjoy the beauty of the huge marble corridors, high arched ceilings, and natural light streaming in from the skylights. But don't let that distract you from the specialty shops (there are more than 100 spread across the three levels) along the main passageways and tucked into side corridors. The merchants include fashions from Ann Taylor and Jos. A. Bank, to Victoria's Secret and H&M. Prepare for walking at Comfort Shoes or 9 West. Stop by Moleskine to purchase a journal to document your travels. There is a branch of Travelex for money exchange and a US Post Office. A food court with all of the usual chains is located on the basement floor.

Southwest Waterfront. The first stage of a multi-year, multi-dimensional development of a derelict area of DC's waterfront includes the first of several upscale shopping areas at The Wharf. With much of the emphasis on residential building, most of the shops focus on the home. Ligne Roset deals with contemporary furnishings, rugs, and textiles; Martha Spak Gallery features artwork. Politics and Prose, Washington's popular independent bookstore on Connecticut Avenue opened a second branch here. When you grow weary of shopping, treat yourself to handmade chocolates from sustainable and fair-trade sources at Harper Macaw.

Museum shops

For the most unique, personal, and memorable gifts or mementoes, visit the shops at museums and galleries, each of which stocks items that reflect the theme of the attraction. Galleries sell everything from coffee-table books to distinctive jewelry and silk scarves. The Air and Space Museum highlights toys and games that engage children's imagination. At the Museum of the American Indian, you'll find bowls, beadwork, and carvings. Collect all of the official White House Christmas tree ornaments at the White House Visitor Center, or a T-shirt defiantly listing the names of banned books at the Library of Congress.

The Arena Stage at the Mead Center for American Theater

ENTERTAINMENT

Washington enjoys an increasingly cosmopolitan arts and music scene. From classic symphonies to band concerts, and classical ballet to edgy experimental theater, visitors will find no shortage of stimulating entertainment.

Where entertainment is concerned, the biggest challenge is winnowing one choice from all of the options. The Going Out Guide in the *Washington Post* (www.washingtonpost.com/goingoutguide) and Things to Do in the *Washingtonian* (www.washingtonian.com/sections/things-to-do) give comprehensive calendars of events. The free *Washington Weekly* – found at corner kiosks – often highlights fringe events that more mainstream media does not cover. LGBT-centric events are found in the *Metro Weekly* (www.metroweekly.com). In all categories, the most comprehensive site to visit is www.culturecapital.com. It has locations (with maps), prices, and useful links.

THEATER

In recent years, Washington has expanded its theatrical realm and is now considered a cultural hub for stage performances. It is now considered one of the top cities in the country for the quality and number of theatrical offerings. Nearly 100 theater companies in Washington and the surrounding Maryland and Virginia counties are listed at www.theatre-washington.org. You'll find everything from venues for touring companies of Broadway shows, resident companies, tiny staged revivals, original and experimental works, and community theaters with part-time thespians. There's a strong base of talent, in part due to the proximity of New York's theatrical world, but a core of well-trained and talented regional and transplanted performers, directors, and technical artists call Washington home. With large immigrant and multicultural populations, you'll find stage companies serving a wide range of special interests.

Increasingly, Washington is the final stop for Broadway-bound productions, with producers respecting the reaction and opinion of DC's audiences. As the center of national and international politics, many productions reflect political and social issues. Be it a contemporary staging of a Shakespeare classic, an original political drama, or a satirical revue, the undercurrent of Washington's raison d'être is in the footlights every night.

DC Jazz Jam, at The Brixton on U Street

MUSIC

In a typical week, music lovers can choose between madrigals by Italian-Jewish composers; a Cole Porter revue; an evening of 20-minute operas; Mexican chamber music; a free performance by the National Symphony Orchestra; and a high-priced concert by the hottest pop star. It's not surprising, given the broad diversity of the population and interests in this cosmopolitan city. Every genre has multiple companies and orchestras that share the common traits of high quality and loyal followings.

Given the image of Washington as the haven of traditional, well-heeled, and often conservative tastes, the popularity of classical music is not surprising. But the city also has a thriving enthusiasm for house music and dance clubs. Jazz's roots reach deeply into Washington's cultural history and it has some of the oldest and most respected jazz clubs in the country. It's considered the choral capital of the country, with performers giving voice in symphonic, chamber ensembles, choirs, and a cappella forms. The arrival of immigrants and refugees adds another dimension to the musical scene as they keep their ethnic identities alive with the songs and instruments from home.

DANCE

DC's dance world is a whirl of classic, ballet, contemporary, avant-garde, and folk movement. In addition to resident dance companies, the city regularly welcomes international performers and touring companies. As its reputation builds, the city has been the site of world premieres. It hosts two annual major festivals, and every cultural celebration features dancers performing in traditional costumes. Audiences can travel the world through dances of India, the Silk Road of central Asia, and Hispanic countries, and enjoy the passion of the tango and the mesmerizing beat of rhythmic dance troupes.

NIGHTLIFE

Despite having a millennial-age population and being a hub for conventions, Washington does not have a rousing nightlife. This is, ultimately, a working town and people must get up and go to work the next day. Having said that, the club scene is as active as any major city, with DJ dance clubs and jazz lounges playing far into the night, especially along the U Street/14th Street corridor in Logan Circle and 18th Street NW in Adams Morgan. The hottest trend is rooftop and balcony bars with customers imbibing while listening to live music and enjoying views of Washington at night. Comedy clubs are another draw after hours, be they improv venues for new and rising comedians or satirical venues that take pointed aim at politicos.

Cycling around the Tidal Basin

SPORTS AND ACTIVITIES

Not all of the action in Washington is on Capitol Hill. A roster of professional sports teams and a wide variety of outdoor activities for almost every interest gives visitors many opportunities to enjoy more of the city's life.

All of the major and most minor professional sports are played in Washington. They are a source of great pride in the city and you'll see the logos of the teams everywhere. For residents, the scope of participatory activities is wide-ranging.

PROFESSIONAL TEAMS

The Nationals are the Major League Baseball team. Their stadium on the Southwest Waterfront is a cornerstone of that area's redevelopment.

The Washington Redskins of the National Football League (American football) consistently draws the highest attendance in the league.

DC United is the professional soccer (football in the rest of the world) team. The sport enjoys a large and growing fan base in the US.

The Washington Wizards are in the National Basketball Association. They play at the Capital One Arena as do The Mystics of the Women's National Basketball Association.

Despite being a 'southern' city, Washington has a professional ice hockey team, the Capitols, more commonly called the Caps.

Professional tennis is represented by the Washington Kastles. It is a co-ed team that plays at the Smith Center in Northwest Washington.

PARTICIPATORY ACTIVITIES

Cycling: Big Wheel Bikes in Georgetown on the C&O Canal towpath offers several rental options (www.bigwheelbikes.com). Bike & Roll has locations at L'Enfant Plaza, Union Station, and the American History Museum. They supply maps of sightseeing routes (www.bikeandrolldc.com). Capital Bikeshare charges by the hour. Even if you rent by the day, you must check in every hour or pay an additional fee (www.capitalbikeshare.com).

Golf: There are three public golf courses. East Potomac has two nine and one 18-hole course; Langston in Northeast DC is the only one with water hazards. Rock Creek's is challenging because of extreme hills and narrow fairways (www.golfdc.com).

Horseback riding: Rock Creek Horse Center offers one-hour guided rides through Rock Creek Park. Rides are limited to four people. Reservations required (www.rockcreekhorsecenter.com).

Joggers on the Mall   *Skating at the National Gallery of Art*

Ice skating: The rink in the National Gallery of Art's Sculpture Garden opens mid-November to mid-March. It's open after dark. Also open during the same period, the rink at Washington Harbor is larger than the Rockefeller Center's. The Canal Park rink on the riverfront is open mid-November through February.

Running\jogging: The Mall is car-free and lit up at night. The C&O Canal in Georgetown has a well-maintained dirt path. Rock Creek Park has paved and off-road trails. The National Arboretum has 10 miles (16km) of trails.

Tennis: The city operates 130 public courts in Washington, most of which are listed on the website of the local tennis league, Tennis DC (www.tennisdc.com).

Water activities: To not take advantage of the Potomac River is to miss part of the Washington Experience. Spirit and Odyssey both operate cruises from The Wharf on the southeast waterfront. Lunch, brunch, themed, and dinner cruises glide past landmarks for three and a half hours (www.spiritcruises.com; www.odysseycruises.com).

DC Ducks offers tours in an amphibious military personnel carrier. Part of the tour is on land; then the Duck splashes into the Potomac to continue the sightseeing from the water (www.dcducks.com).

The Water Taxi (www.potomacriverboatcompany.com) operates from The Wharf to Georgetown, Alexandria, and National Harbor. During the season, it provides a water taxi service to the Nationals stadium. For sightseeing, try DC Cruises (www.dc-cruises.com), which has happy hour, nighttime, and fall foliage tours.

Rent paddleboats at the Tidal Basin in the summer (see page 48). Kayaks, canoes, and SUPs are available at Key Bridge Boathouse. Thompson Boat Center in Georgetown rents SUPs as well as hydrobikes (www.boatingdc.com). At the Wharf, there's a sailing school and watersport equipment rental (www.dcsail.com).

Redskins controversy

A bitter debate surrounds the name of the Washington American football team. Called the Redskins, it is considered a racial slur against Native Americans.

The team was named by its original owner, George P. Marshall, who claimed it was to honor the first coach and several players who were Native Americans. However, others say that Marshall was far from an enlightened individual and that he used the term derisively.

Public pressure has not swayed the current owner or fans into considering a name change. Legal efforts to force a change through interpretations of federal trademark laws prohibiting derogatory labeling have also failed.

When polled, most Native Americans say they are more concerned about problems facing their tribal nations, like substandard schools, unemployment, and health issues than they are about the team's name.

Georgetown and Federal City in 1801

HISTORY: KEY DATES

Washington's inception was itself an historical event, as it was created as the seat of a new nation. Since then, it has continued to be at the center of memorable and influential incidents.

EARLY YEARS AND CIVIC GROWTH

1783	Treaty of Paris brings the American Revolution to an end.
1789	US Constitution is ratified.
1790–91	Maryland and Virginia give up land for the new capital. Pierre L'Enfant lays out his plan for the city.
1799	Death of George Washington.
1800	John Adams is the first president to occupy the White House.
1814	The British set fire to the White House and Capitol during the War of 1812–15.
1835	The Baltimore and Ohio Railroad reaches the city.
1850	Construction of the Chesapeake and Ohio Canal is completed. Congress abolishes the slave trade in the District, but owning slaves remains legal.
1861	The Civil War begins. Washington is inside Maryland, a southern-sympathizing state kept in the Union by occupation of Federal forces.
1863	Lincoln issues the Emancipation Proclamation. The US Capitol is completed.
1865	The Civil War Ends. Lincoln is assassinated.
1868	The 14th Amendment, granting citizenship to all persons born in the US, including former slaves, passes.
1884	The Washington Monument is completed.
1897	The Library of Congress opens.

WORLD WARS

1917	US enters World War I.
1918	World War I ends.
1920	US women gain the right to vote. The 18th Amendment, which prohibits alcoholic beverages, takes effect.

Donald Trump's inauguration

1922	Lincoln Memorial is dedicated.
1933	Prohibition (the 18th Amendment) is repealed.
1941	US enters World War II. The National Airport and National Gallery of Art open.
1945	World War II ends.

THE BOOMER YEARS

1963	Martin Luther King Jr. delivers his 'I Have a Dream' speech at the Lincoln Memorial in front of 200,000 people.
1968	Riots erupt following the assassination of Dr. King. Twelve people die.
1972	Burglars break into the Democratic Party headquarters at the Watergate. The ensuing saga ends with President Nixon's resignation.
1976	The Metrorail opens its first subway route.
1982	The Vietnam Memorial is unveiled.
1993	The Vietnam Women's Memorial and United States Holocaust Memorial Museum open.
1999	President Bill Clinton is impeached by the House of Representatives, but acquitted by the Senate.

THE 21ST CENTURY

2001	Terrorists crash a hijacked plane into the Pentagon, killing 189.
2002	Two snipers terrorize the DC area for three weeks, killing 10 in random attacks.
2004	World War II Memorial is dedicated. National Museum of the American Indian opens.
2008	Barack Obama becomes the first African American president.
2010	Massive blizzard buries the city in 2.5ft (0.7 meters) of snow. First same sex marriage is performed in the District.
2011	Martin Luther King. Jr. Monument dedicated. Occupy Wall Street demonstrators build tent city on the Mall.
2016	National Museum of African American History and Culture opens. DC voters approve referendum on statehood by 86 percent. Congress ignores the results.
2017	Donald Trump sworn in as president. Women's March on Washington. March for Science takes place in Washington and 600 other cities. Resist movement starts in National Park Service.

BEST ROUTES

The White House seen from Lafayette Square

THE WHITE HOUSE AND ENVIRONS

It's arguably the most famous address in the world: 1600 Pennsylvanian Avenue, and photos of its north-facing facade are instantly recognizable. The White House is a symbol of the president and the country he represents.

DISTANCE: 1.5 miles (2.5km)
TIME: An easy half-day
START: North end of LaFayette Square
END: Renwick Gallery
POINTS TO NOTE: The nearest Metro stations are Farragut West (Yellow and Blue lines), McPherson Square (Yellow and Blue lines) and Metro Center (Red line). The DC Circulator bus stops at Georgetown-Union Station (Yellow line) and Woodley Park-McPherson Station (Green line). You will need to walk three or four blocks from each Metro or bus stop to LaFayette Square.

This is a comfortable stroll around a famous piece of real estate. Plan on spending an hour or so at the Visitor Center; take selfies at the south lawn of the White House; savor the moment as you stand on the Ellipse with the White House behind you, the Washington Monument in front of you, and the Jefferson Memorial beyond. Then enjoy the work of creative minds on display at the Renwick Gallery.

Until the end of World War II, citizens could stroll into the White House and shake hands with the president. No more. Security is very tight in the vicinity of the White House, which can be disconcerting. Operate on the assumption that if the security officers seem relaxed, you have nothing to worry about.

LAFAYETTE SQUARE

The famous view of the north facade of the White House is seen from **LaFayette Square ❶** (H Street NW between 15th and 17th streets), the closest you will get to the White House. Pennsylvania Avenue, at the south end of the square, has been closed to both vehicular and pedestrian traffic for years, except for prearranged tours. In the past, the square was a popular spot where tourists posed for photos and demonstrators congregated. Sadly, security concerns have made it off-limits and it is heavily patrolled by various police agencies.

Built in 1815, every president since James Madison has attended at least one service at **St John's Episco-**

St. John's Episcopal Church

pal Church ❷ (corner of H Street NW and 16th Street; www.stjohns-dc.org). Pew 54 is the 'President's Pew' and is reserved for the president's use. The bell was cast by Paul Revere's son in 1822 in his Boston foundry. For many years, it not only called worshippers to services but also was an alarm bell for the city. The stained glass windows from Chartres, in France, depict scenes from the Gospel of St John and the window above the altar is a unique rendition of the Last Sup-

per. Tours are given following the Sunday morning service.

On leaving the church, head east along H Street then turn right onto 15th Street. The large neoclassical building on your right is the Department of the Treasury. The statue in front is of Alexander Hamilton, the first Secretary of the Treasury. If the building looks vaguely familiar, that's because it is on the back of the $10 bill. Like the White House, it was burned by the British in 1814. The Treasury Department caused a stir during those years when women were hired to fill clerical positions vacated by men who left to fight in the Union Army. These were the first female federal employees. They hand-cut paper money, which was another innovation introduced during the war.

A bit farther along, **Old Ebbitt Grill**, see ❶, is a good stop for lunch or dinner and has a children's menu, while **Pinea**, see ❷, serves upscale classic Mediterranean dishes.

WHITE HOUSE VISITOR CENTER

Continue south on 15th Street to the **White House Visitor Center** ❸ (1401

The Blue Room

Pennsylvania Avenue NW; www.nps.gov/whho; daily 7.40am–4pm; free). Note that there are two Pennsylvania Avenues that intersect 15th Street. Ignore the first one and continue to the intersection of E Street and Pennsylvania Avenue. To your left you will see the blue awnings of the visitor center.

It is very difficult to get on a tour of the White House. Requests can be submitted up to three months (but no less than 21 days) in advance and places are allocated on a first come, first served basis. This must be done through your congressional representative. Foreign nationals should contact their country's embassy. The self-guiding tours last around 20 minutes and take in the public rooms in the East Wing: the Blue Room, Red Room, Green Room, State Dining Room, the China Room, and the Rose Garden.

If you can't get on a tour, the Visitor Center is a good substitute. It is filled with engaging displays about the history of the building and the people who have called it home, plus interesting, and sometimes befuddling, gifts from foreign powers.

THE ELLIPSE

On leaving the Visitor Center, go west to cross 15th Street and enter the grounds of the **Ellipse ❹**. From here you have a clear view of both the White House South Lawn and the Washington Monument and the Jefferson Memorial to the south. You'll pass the spot where the National Christmas Tree is placed each year; a smaller evergreen tree fills the space outside of holiday season. The Zero Milestone close by marks the point at which distances from Washington are measured.

The entire 82 acres (33 hectares) of parks and lawns surrounding the White House are officially part of the National Park Service. A permanent crew of arborists, landscape architects, and gardeners tend the White House lawn – a showcase of 500 trees, 4,000 flowering shrubs, and 12 acres (5 hectares) of manicured lawn.

Continue west the turn right onto 17th Street. The distinctive building on your right is the Eisenhower Executive Office Building, which houses the Office of the

Public events

The annual Easter Egg Roll began in the 1870s, when children would roll Easter eggs and themselves down Capitol Hill. Grouchy Congressmen complained that the lawn was being damaged and banned the fun, but President Rutherford B. Hayes invited children to the White House instead and the tradition has continued since then. Tickets are awarded by lottery. You should apply well in advance.

Twice a year, the White House Garden opens its gates to the public. The autumn and spring tours (dates vary) include the Rose Garden, Jacqueline Kennedy Garden, and Kitchen Garden. Timed, free tickets are awarded on the day from a National Park Service tent www.nps.gov/whho.

White House Visitor Center   *Renwick Gallery*

Vice President. Built between 1871 and 1888, its French Second Empire architecture was originally criticized, but it is now considered one of the most elegant buildings in Washington. President Eisenhower held the first televised presidential news conference here in 1955; President Nixon had his primary office in the building, preferring to use the Oval Office only for ceremonial occasions.

THE RENWICK GALLERY

The **Renwick Gallery ❺** (Pennsylvania Avenue and 17th Street; daily 10am–5.30pm; free) is one of the Smithsonian museums and focuses on American craft and decorative art from the 19th to 21st century. Known as the 'American Louvre', it was built in 1859 to display William Corcoran's collection of European and American art. The building was later used for government offices and in poor repair when Jacqueline Kennedy intervened to prevent it from being demolished. It is worth visiting just to see the Grand Staircase.

Pennsylvania Avenue across 17th Street has a string of restaurants that cater to office workers and tourists. **The Exchange Saloon**, see ❸, is DC's oldest sports bar, while **GCDC**, see ❹, serves classic grilled cheese sandwiches, tater tots, and other comfort food.

Food and Drink

❶ OLD EBBITT GRILL

675 15th Street, NW; www.ebbitt.com; $$
The place opened as a saloon and boarding house in 1859 and has been feeding notables and visitors alike ever since. It's particularly known for the oyster bar, but they also cater to kids.

❷ PINEA

515 15th Street, NW; www.pineadc.com; $$$
This is an elegant spot for Mediterranean fare, with unusual wines and craft cocktails. Dishes use citrus and fragrant ingredients like lavender and rosemary. The spacious dining room is light-filled and comfortable.

❸ THE EXCHANGE SALOON

1719 G Street, NW; www.theexchangesaloon.com; $$
DC's oldest sports bar caters to visitors who cannot bear to miss their home team's games, with 26 flat screen HDTV monitors and state-of-the-art sound system. It serves typical sports bar fare: sandwiches, salads, and a nice selection of beers.

❹ GCDC

1730 Pennsylvania Avenue, NW; www.grilledcheesedc.com; $
DC's only grilled cheese bar, serving classic and creative takes on a basic comfort food for lunch and dinner. Gluten-free options are available. They offer wine, beer, and cocktail pairing for the sandwiches. Great for families.

The US Capitol Building

CAPITOL HILL

The embodiment of two branches of government, the largest storehouse of knowledge in the world, the Bard's first folio, a tribute to Women's Rights, and gardens in bloom year-round make for a very full day around Capitol Hill.

DISTANCE: 2 miles (3km)
TIME: A comfortable full day
START: US Capitol Visitor Center
END: Grant's Statue (west face of the Capitol)
POINTS TO NOTE: Capitol Hill is a 10-minute walk from Capitol South (Orange, Silver, and Blue lines) and Union Station (Red Line). The DC Circulator bus stops at National Mall (red route); Union Station-Navy Yard (blue route). Expect to spend several hours at the Capitol and at least an hour at the Library of Congress. The Supreme Court takes most visitors about an hour, as does the Women's Equality Monument and Folger Library. The Library of Congress has maps of the building with suggestions as to what to see depending on how much time you have. The Capitol and Library of Congress are both good places for children and the guides know how to keep kids engaged in the history; the Botanical Garden has kids' areas and activities. While the tour itself is not that long, you will do a lot of walking in the buildings.

The few blocks around 'The Hill' hold some of the most influential establishments in the country, if not the world. Congress and the Supreme Court meet here; the Library of Congress needs three buildings to contain its massive holdings; the Folger Shakespeare Library has the world's most extensive collection of Shakespeare's works and academia; while the Belmont-Paul Women's Equality National Memorial reminds visitors of the struggle for women's right to vote. The United States Botanical Garden is a refreshing and relaxing way to cap off this busy tour.

Before you do anything else, stop and take a long look at the **US Capitol Building ❶** (www.visitthecapitol.gov; Visitor Center Mon–Sat 8.30am–4.30pm; free). It's so familiar from photos that its neoclassical beauty is often overlooked.

Pierre L'Enfant described the only hill in the confines of the planned city as 'a pedestal waiting for a superstructure', and the Capitol certainly fits his vision. George Washington himself chose the design of an amateur architect, Dr William Thornton, for its 'grandeur' and 'sim-

The US Capitol Building's Rotunda

plicity'. Construction started in 1793, and congress met there for the first time in 1800. During the War of 1812, the British torched what British Admiral George Cockburn called 'this harbor of Yankee democracy', but repairs and expansion continued unabated, even during the Civil War. Lincoln said that 'if people see the Capitol is going on… it is a sign we intend that the Union shall go on'. Today, nearly 20,000 staff members, lobbyists, and journalists swarm like bees around the Capitol hive.

Entry is permitted by guided tour. Places can be booked online up to three months in advance through the office of your congressional representative or the Capitol Hill website. Foreign nationals should contact their embassy. A limited number of same-day entry passes are available, but it is best to arrive early to avoid waiting in line for a long time. In addition to the primary tour, there are other tours of the Capitol and its grounds, some of which are advertised inside the visitor center, the entrance to which is located next to the steps on the east side of the building.

If you want to see congress in session, you need a gallery pass. It is best to arrange this in advance through your congressional representative. Otherwise, you must go to reception and contact the appropriate office, and then go to the office and collect the pass. Foreign nationals can simply show their passport or other photo ID at reception.

Visitors assemble for the tour in a lobby filled with statues of significant Americans donated by individual states. From there, they are guided into the main lobby of the building. A simple plaque on the wall is the memorial to passengers and crew of Flight 93, the plane that crashed in Shanksville, PA on 9/11 when passengers tried to overwhelm its hijackers. It is believed that the plane's ultimate target was the Capitol.

The awesome, magnificent beauty of the lobby under the great rotunda of the Capitol Dome is overwhelming. You are enveloped in an aura of history and power, surrounded by statues of 20th-century presidents and statesmen and women. Above you, Constantino Brumidi's *Apotheosis of Washington* depicts the first

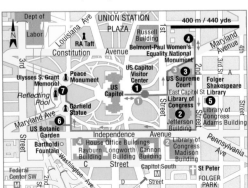

The Library of Congress

president and other colonial dignitaries mingling with allegorical figures in a classical motif. The frieze around the base of the dome depicts 400 years of American history. If you have sharp eyes, you might recognize some of the people scurrying through the rotunda and hallways as representatives and senators, en route from meetings to their offices.

One area where they don't spend time chatting is the Statuary Hall. A quirk of the semicircular shape and domed ceiling amplifies the slightest sound. Even when the area is filled with people, every whisper carries across the room, something politicians avoid.

After the tour, take time to visit the permanent exhibit. It's far less imposing, but fills in gaps that the guided tour cannot demonstrate. A series of dioramas show DC's growth over the centuries, short films explain the Bill of Rights and other important foundations of government, and a touchscreen game tests your knowledge of government. There is also the crypt where congress planned to inter George Washington, but as he decreed that he and his wife Martha be buried at Mount Vernon, the crypt remains empty.

The **US Capitol Restaurant**, see ❶, is open for breakfast and lunch.

LIBRARY OF CONGRESS

The **Library of Congress** ❷ (101 Independence Avenue SE; www.loc.gov; Mon–Sat 10am–5.30pm; free; self-guiding tours available in 12 languages; one-

hour tours Mon–Fri 10.30am–3.30pm; family tours, suitable for 6–12-year-olds, available during peak visitation periods) can be accessed by means of an underground passageway from the Capitol or through the entrance on Independence Avenue.

The original library was housed in the Capitol and was intended only for the use of legislators. It was destroyed in a fire ignited by the British in 1814. Thomas Jefferson subsequently sold his personal library to Congress but the collection quickly outgrew its Capitol home. A second fire in 1851 (caused by a faulty fireplace flue) reduced the collection to ashes. Congress allocated funds for a new building, which opened in 1897.

The library now has over 150 million books, rare manuscripts, maps, musical scores, recordings, films, photographs, 100,000 comic books, the stockpile of Bob Hope's jokes, a Gutenberg Bible, drafts of the Declaration of Independence and the Gettysburg Address, and the oldest known written tablet which dates from 2040 BC. It is the largest collection of written, illustrated, and recorded knowledge in the world.

The library encompasses three buildings, but the one open to the public is the magnificent Thomas Jefferson Building. The Great Hall is two stories of white marble ascending 75ft (23 meters) presided over by a marble mosaic of Minerva, the goddess of wisdom.

Few rooms in all of Washington are more impressive than the Main Reading

Library of Congress dome   *The Supreme Court*

Room. Researchers work in a room with a 160ft (49-meter) -high domed ceiling that displays murals showing the great ages of Western civilization, all gold-leafed and hand-painted with clusters of richly veined marble columns. Above all of this, in a stained glass cupola illuminated by sunlight, there's a statue of a winsome female who depicts the principle of human understanding.

The **Madison Café**, see ②, is open to the public.

THE SUPREME COURT

With only nine justices, the **Supreme Court** ❸ (1st Street and East Capitol Street NE; www.supremecourt.gov; Mon–Fri 9am–4.30pm; free) is the smallest branch of the federal government, yet its rulings have a profound impact on American society and law. For the first 145 years, the court had no permanent home, meeting in taverns, hotels, private residences, and the Capitol itself. The court's permanent home was completed in 1935.

The details on the building show the givers of law, including Moses and Confucius, and legal figures like John Marshall and William Howard Taft as young, virile men. The famous quote over the entrance 'Equal Justice Under Law' is not wisdom from a famous legal mind. The architect coined the statement because it fit the available space.

Don't miss the 24-minute orientation film. Its most interesting features are comments by present and past justices on the workings of the court and the thought processes of the justices. Even if you do not always agree with their decisions, you will have a new respect for the responsibility they have and which they recognize. The permanent displays are about the history of the court, illustrious judges, and important rulings.

The **Supreme Court Cafeteria**, see ❸, serves light meals and entrees.

EAST OF THE CAPITOL

Directly across the street from the north exit of the Supreme Court Building lies the **Belmont-Paul Women's Equality National Monument** ❹ (144 Constitution Avenue NE; www.nps.gov/bepa; daily 9am–5pm; limited opening hours in winter, see website for details; guided tours 9.30am, 11am, 2pm, and 3.30pm; free). Alice Paul and Alva Belmont were leading figures in the suffrage movement. This building was home to the National Women's Party for nearly 90 years and was the epicenter of the fight for women's rights. Displays and photographs tell the story of the suffrage movement, an often violent and bloody struggle which culminated in the successful passage of the 19th Amendment, which gave women the right to vote.

To reach the **Folger Shakespeare Library** ❺ (201 East Capitol Street NE; www.folger.edu; Mon–Sat 10am–5pm, Sun noon–5pm; guided tours Mon–Sat 11am, 1pm, and 3pm, Sun noon and 3pm; Reading Room tour Sat noon; gar-

The Great Hall, Folger Shakespeare Library

Southwest Waterfront

The latest area to catch the eye of developers and real estate investors is Washington's Southwest Waterfront, about seven blocks south of the National Mall and Capitol Hill. Long neglected, with empty lots, derelict buildings, and low-income housing, it is now seeing glitzy, expensive gentrification.

The renaissance started with the opening of the Nationals' Stadium, home of Washington's Major League Baseball team, the Nationals (aka The Nats). That was followed in 2017 by the opening of The Wharf, an upscale hotel, retail, and residential complex on the Potomac River. It compliments a marina which was already there and which docks the dinner cruise boats and private vessels. It is also a stop for water taxis that ferry passengers upriver to Georgetown and across the river to Alexandria.

Arena Stage, one of DC's professional theaters, is here, as is The Anthem, a performance, conference, and concert venue that can hold 6,000 people.

A decidedly unglitzy but fun spot just north of The Wharf is the Maine Street Fish Market. Opened in 1805, the open air stands display the catch of the day on huge mounds of shaved ice. You can do a lot worse than order a carry out meal of fried fish and slaw, follow the riverside boardwalk to the public park at the other end of the development, and have a picnic by the river.

den tours Apr–Oct Sat 10am; free) head south down 2nd Street NE to the corner of East Capitol Street NE. The library's exterior is more Washington neoclassical architecture, but inside, Will himself would feel at home. It's pure Tudor England, with oak paneling, ornamental floor tiles, and high plaster ceilings. The Folger houses the world's largest collection of Shakespeare's printed works, including a set of priceless First Folios from 1623. The guided tour takes you into the Great Hall, where many of the treasures are displayed. The Folger Theater stages plays of the era and performances of Renaissance and medieval music. The garden is planted with herbs and flowers from Shakespeare's time.

US BOTANIC GARDEN

From the Folger Library, continue south on 2nd Street then turn right onto Independence Avenue. The buildings you pass on your left as you walk down Independence Avenue contain the offices of members of Congress. There is a **Subway** sandwich shop inside the Rayburn House Office Building, see ❹. Opposite the Garden Conservatory and adjacent to the RHOB is the Bartholdi Park. Anchored by a lovely fountain, it presents gardening on a scale suitable for home landscapes.

From here head north up 1st Street; the entrance to the **United States Botanic Garden** ❻ (1st Street and Maryland Avenue SW; www.usbg.gov; daily 10am–5pm, walk-in tours dependent

National Botanical Garden   *Ulyssess S. Grant Memorial*

on docent availability, check website for details of special tours; free cell phone tours available on 202-730-9303; free) is on your left. The plaza has shaded tables during the summer.

The garden was originally established for specimen plants brought back from South America and the Pacific by the Wilkes Exhibition in 1842. As the collection expanded, a conservatory was added, which now includes a huge glass atrium and over 65,000 plants. The indoor conservatory and atrium has 11 environments from across the globe. The center of the atrium is an above-ground walkway through a tropical rain forest. Outside, the 3-acre (1.2-hectare) National Garden features plants of the mid-Atlantic, a Rose Garden, a Butterfly Garden, and the First Ladies' Water Garden.

ULYSSES S. GRANT MEMORIAL

Thirty years after the Battle of Appomattox, veterans of the Union Army began soliciting funds for a memorial to the general and two-term president, Ulysses S. Grant. The largest equestrian statue in the world, the **Ulysses S. Grant Memorial** ❼ (www.aoc.gov/grant) shows a twice life-sized Grant sitting resolutely on his horse while sculptures on either side of him depict cavalry and artillery troops in battle. The sculptures are notable for their attention to detail in the realistic trappings and uniforms, the faces of the soldiers, and the horses' bodies.

Food and Drink

❶ US CAPITOL RESTAURANT
Lower Level, US Capitol Building; $
Open for a continental breakfast and full lunch, this is a cafeteria-style restaurant with seating for several hundred people. There are many food stations serving hot meals, salads, and sandwiches. Food allergies cannot be accommodated.

❷ MADISON CAFÉ
Madison Building, Library of Congress; www.loc.gov/visit/dining; $
This is a basic grill and grab-and-go, used more for staff and researchers than for visitors, since it is not in the main building tourists visit. It serves made-to-order grilled items, coffee, and sodas.

❸ SUPREME COURT CAFETERIA
First Floor, Supreme Court Building; www.supremecourt.gov; $
A surprisingly nice cafeteria that is rarely crowded. There's a full selection of hot and cold lunch items, plus breakfast available from 7.30am. It's nothing fancy as far as ambiance goes, but it's convenient and well priced.

❹ SUBWAY
Rayburn Building; $
You might rub shoulders with members of Congress grabbing a quick sandwich at this branch of the sandwich chain. More likely, it will be members of their staff or tourists.

THE WAR MEMORIALS

The western reach of the National Mall along the Reflecting Pool is one of the most visited areas of Washington. As the memorials that line it honor veterans, patriots, and two presidents, it is also one of the most solemn.

DISTANCE: 1.5 miles (2.5km)

TIME: Plan to spend two hours on this tour. It invites a slow passage, with time to absorb the history and sacrifice that the memorials represent.

START: The Washington Monument

END: DC War Memorial

POINTS TO NOTE: Consider visiting at night or very early in the morning, when it's cooler and the crowds are few. Metro stations Federal Triangle and Smithsonian (Blue, Orange, and Silver lines) are nearby, as is the DC Connector bus Mall stop (red route). You can combine this tour with the Tidal Basin Monuments walk (see page 46), approximately 2 miles (3km), which makes for a very long half-day and a lot of walking. There are no restaurants along this route. There is a kiosk selling sandwiches and drinks between the Lincoln Memorial and the Korean War Memorial. You'll also find vans selling water and snacks near the Washington Monument and Lincoln Memorial and both sights have restrooms.

The Washington Monument stands at the eastern end of the Reflecting Pool and the Lincoln Memorial at the western end, tributes to two of the most famous and influential Americans. Between them are memorials to the unknown men and women who served the nation in times of war. The area has seen many demonstrations, which usually extend to the National Mall, to the east of the Washington Monument. Perhaps the most famous is Martin Luther King Jr's 'I Have a Dream' speech in 1963. Delivered on the steps of the Lincoln Memorial, it is considered a defining moment in the Civil Rights Movement. Huge protests against the Vietnam War and the 'Occupy' movement against corporate practices also used the area.

On most days, however, the only protestors you will encounter are the ducks and geese in the Reflecting Pool who seem annoyed that tourists are not allowed to feed them.

THE WASHINGTON MONUMENT

Perhaps the most recognized of Washington's monuments, the **Washington**

The Washington Monument

Monument ❶ (www.nps.gov/wamo; daily 24hrs) boasts the best view of the city from atop its tower. Unfortunately, you may not be able to enjoy the view. The 555ft (169-meter) -high monument was closed after the 2011 earthquake. The 5.8 quake cracked the monument and raised serious concerns about its stability. No sooner had it reopened than problems developed with the elevator. A private philanthropist is donating the money for the project, but the National Park Service also wants to improve a new security entrance and for that congress must authorize the funds. It will be 2019 at the earliest before the monument reopens.

Originally, the monument was to be an imposing equestrian statue, but the congress never got around to allocating the money. Finally a group of private citizens raised $28,000 for the memorial. The cornerstone for the more modest

and distinct obelisk was laid on July 4, 1848, but construction was delayed, in part by the Civil War, and also by questions about the allocation of the money that was raised.

Private donations of stones from states, organizations, and other countries helped get the work started again. Often, those were inscribed with mottoes and good wishes, though not all were appreciated. One stone, donated by Pope Pius IX provoked anti-Catholic protestors to smash the stone and throw the pieces into the Potomac River. The work was finally completed and the monument dedicated in 1888.

You'll notice that the stones change shade partway up the shaft, marking the switch from Maryland to Massachusetts marble when the work resumed. When the discrepancy was noticed, work stopped until a more compatible quarry was found.

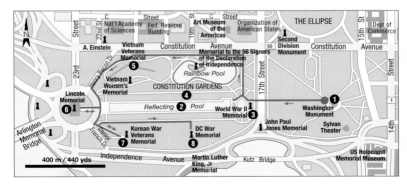

National World War II Memorial

LINCOLN MEMORIAL REFLECTING POOL

Immediately to the west of the monument is the **Lincoln Memorial Reflecting Pool** ❷. It's 2,029ft (618 meters) long and 167ft (51 meters) wide and is about 24in (0.6 meters) deep. Lined by walking paths, it is a familiar stroll, popular with tourists, joggers, and dog-walkers. In recent years, it has been subject to a series of disasters, with damage from the construction of the National World War II Memorial, and various parasites and algae.

NATIONAL WORLD WAR II MEMORIAL

The **National World War II Memorial** ❸ (www.nps.gov/wwii; daily 24hrs) honors the 16 million men and women who served in the armed forces, the 400,000 who died, and the civilians who waited and worked on the home front. Dedicated on Memorial Day, 2004, more than 4.5 million people visit the memorial every year. Many of them are aged veterans and their families.

The memorial was designed by Friedrich St Florian who wanted to evoke classic European triumphant memorials. It consists of 56 pillars and a pair of triumphal arches arranged in a semicircle around a plaza and fountain. The pillars are engraved with the 48 states that were part of the country in 1945, plus the Territories of Alaska and Hawaii, the Commonwealth of the Philippines, Puerto Rico, Guam, American Samoa, and the US Virgin Islands. Each pillar has an oak and a wheat laurel wreath. The oak symbolizes military and industrial strength, while the wheat recognizes the US's role as the breadbasket for other countries during the war. The two arches, one label 'Atlantic' and the other 'Pacific' are topped with laurel wreaths suspended in the air and carried by four eagles.

As you approach the memorial from the east, you walk along two walls that show scenes of the war in bas relief. On the side nearest the Pacific arch, the scenes are of a recruit's life: physical exams, taking the oath, getting equipment, battle, burying the dead, and returning home. On the Atlantic side, the scenes include preparing for air and sea assaults in England, and US and Russian troops shaking hands in Germany. Sharp-eyed visitors can look for two images of the iconic 'Kilroy was here' graffiti popular with GIs during World War II.

A separate Freedom Wall near the monument has 4,048 gold stars, one for every 100 Americans who died, and the motto 'Here we mark the price of freedom'.

CONSTITUTION GARDENS

Head north from the memorial, then turn left to follow the path that borders a small lake. Known as Constitution Gar-

Vietnam Veterans Memorial

dens, this swath of green was dedicated in 1976 as part of the Bicentennial Celebration. It is a tranquil setting of shady trees and bench-lined paths that meander along the lake. A small island in the lake holds the **Memorial to the 56 Signers of the Declaration of Independence** ❹ (www.nps.gov/coga; daily 24hrs). Their signatures as they appear on the Declaration are on granite markers in a semicircle.

VIETNAM VETERANS MEMORIAL

The 2-acre (1-hectare) site of the **Vietnam Veterans Memorial** ❺ (www.nps.gov/vive; daily 24hrs) honors the service members who served during the Vietnam Era. It consists of three separate areas: the Vietnam Women's Memorial, the Vietnam Veterans Memorial, and The Three Soldiers statue. Over 3 million people visit the memorial each year. If you grew up during this era, served, or know someone who did, it can be a heart-wrenching experience.

Vietnam Women's Memorial

As you approach the area from the east, you first reach the **Vietnam Women's Memorial**. It is the first monument in Washington, and one of the few in the US, to recognize women's service. During the Vietnam era, 265,000 women volunteered. About 11,000 of them were stationed in Vietnam; most were nurses. Eight servicewomen died while serving in Vietnam. The sculpture portrays three women, two of whom care for a wounded soldier while another gazes skyward, her arms outstretched as though in supplication.

Vietnam Veterans Memorial

Often referred to as 'The Wall', the **Vietnam Veterans Memorial** itself is a stark slash in the earth, most of it below ground level. It starts with a tapered, narrow point, widening as moves midpoint then tapering again. Architect Maya Lin wanted to symbolize the wound that Vietnam created and its gradual healing. At its highest, the wall is 10ft (3 meters) high. Inscribed on it are the names of over 58,000 servicemen and women who died or are listed as missing. The names are listed in chronological order, moving from the westernmost panel eastward. Those killed in action are designated by a diamond, while those listed as missing are marked by a cross. When the death of a missing person is confirmed, a diamond is superimposed over the cross.

Since the Wall was dedicated, over 400,000 items have been left at its base, which no one had expected. Letters, dog tags, photographs, a football helmet, sneakers, a baby's knitted sweater, teddy bears, birthday cards, and even a motorcycle have been left at the Wall. Sometimes there are letters to the serviceman or woman associated with the object. Often there is nothing to indicate who left it or to whom. The Park Service has begun collecting and

Lincoln Memorial

cataloging the memorials and the Vietnam Veterans Memorial Fund plans to construct an education center near the Wall and display many of the remembrances. There is a virtual collection of the items at www.vvmf.org. Near the memorial, there is a kiosk with directions for finding names on the wall.

The Three Soldiers

Frederick Hart's statue of three soldiers gazing toward the wall was added to the Memorial in 1982, two years after the Wall was dedicated. It was an answer to critics of the memorial who felt that the design was symbolic of a grave and shame and not of the patriotism and honor of those who served. Initially it was to be placed close to the Wall, but architect Maya Lin objected. As a compromise, the statue was moved some distance away. In retrospect, this distance adds to the poignancy of the statue, as the three soldiers – one Caucasian, one African American, and one Hispanic – look toward the names of their fallen friends from a distance of increasing time.

A small memorial plaque stands near this statue. It has the names of soldiers who died after the Vietnam War from injuries they suffered during the conflict.

THE LINCOLN MEMORIAL

Continue farther west and you'll reach the incomparable shrine to Abraham Lincoln, the **Lincoln Memorial** ❻

(daily 24hrs; www.nps.gov/linc). Architect Henry Bacon designed the temple-like building, which bears a strong resemblance to Athens' Parthenon. The building is fronted by 36 Doric columns, representing the number of American states at the time of Lincoln's assassination. Above them is a frieze with the 48 states that were in the Union when the Memorial was dedicated on Memorial Day in 1922. On the north and south walls, there are excerpts from his Second Inaugural Address and the Gettysburg Address. Above them are murals by Jules Guerin, which depict guiding principles of Lincoln's life.

Daniel Chester French sculpted the statue of Lincoln seated inside the memorial. If the oversized Lincoln were to stand, he would measure 28ft (8.5 meters) tall. When it was discovered that Lincoln's naturally-lit face was permanently left in shadow, General Electric was called in to install artificial lighting to create the shadows on his hair, brows, cheeks, and chin. Adding a personal touch, French, who had a deaf son and who knew American Sign Language, so shaped Lincoln's hands that the left holds the sign for 'A' and the right 'L'.

At the dedication, the key speaker, Dr Robert Moton, the African American President of Tuskegee Institute, was ushered away after his address and seated in the segregated black section across the road. In 1939, operatic

Korean War Memorial   *DC War Memorial*

singer Marian Anderson, denied permission to perform at the Daughters of the American Revolution Constitution Hall because she was black, sang for an audience of 75,000 at the memorial. Most famously, this was the site of Martin Luther King Jr's 'I Have a Dream' speech.

KOREAN WAR VETERANS MEMORIAL

The **Korean War Veterans Memorial** ❼ (www.nps.gov/kowa; daily 24hrs) commemorates the Americans and those from other nations who served in the often marginalized Korean War. The memorial has several parts. The Mural Wall has 41 panels with more than 2,400 pictures showing marines, navy, army, air force, and coast guard personnel and their equipment. The mural wall of black granite is sandblasted with images of sea, air, and support troops. The reflections represent 38 soldiers, 38 months of fighting, and the 38th parallel that separates the two Korean nations.

Opposite the wall is the United Nations Wall, a low wall that borders the site and lists the 22 nations of the UN that participated in combat or medical operations during the war. A Pool of Remembrance is lined with the numbers of killed, wounded, missing in action, and prisoners of war from all nations. A nearby plaque reads 'Our nation honors her sons and daughters who answered the call to defend a country they never knew and a people they never met'.

But it is the center of the monument that is particularly compelling. Nineteen statues depict a platoon on patrol, dressed in full combat gear and wearily trudging through a landscape of granite and juniper bushes that represents the rugged terrain of Korea. Their ponchos seem to wave in an unseen, cold wind. Several of the soldiers appear to be looking toward the Mural Wall. The monument is particularly poignant at night, when it is lit from below and shadows play on the statues.

THE DC WAR MEMORIAL

Much smaller than the other memorials and somewhat hidden in a grove of trees, the **DC War Memorial** ❽ (www.nps.gov/nama; daily 24hrs) honors the residents of the District who died during World War I. The circular, open-air structure looks like a marble bandstand, because that is what it is. The designers made it large enough for the US Marine Corps Band to fit inside. Their intention was that every concert given there would be a tribute to the fallen.

The building stands on a circular marble platform that is inscribed with the names of the 499 men from Washington who died in the war. It is the only District-specific memorial on the Mall.

Martin Luther King, Jr Memorial

TIDAL BASIN MONUMENTS

One of the loveliest spots in Washington, the Tidal Basin is surrounded by the famous cherry trees and memorials to Thomas Jefferson, George Mason, and Martin Luther King, Jr, and the United States Holocaust Memorial Museum.

DISTANCE: 1.5 miles (2.5km)
TIME: A half-day. If you decide to rent paddleboats on the Tidal Basin, this could be an all-day excursion.
START: Martin Luther King, Jr Memorial
END: United States Holocaust Memorial Museum
POINTS TO NOTE: The nearest Metro stop is Smithsonian (Blue, Orange, and Silver lines). The DC Circulator bus Mall Route (red route) stops at the United States Holocaust Memorial Museum, the Martin Luther King, Jr and Jefferson memorials, and the National Bureau of Engraving and Printing. This tour can be combined with the War Memorials tour (see page 40), which would lengthen it to 3 miles (5km) – a long way in summer. There are restrooms at all of the memorials and there may be trucks selling drinks and snacks along the Tidal Basin near 15th Street. The National Bureau of Engraving and Printing is good for school-age children, but the United States Holocaust Memorial Museum is decidedly not for younger children.

This walk presents many US ideals. Jefferson penned the Declaration of Independence; Madison is responsible for the Bill of Rights; King was instrumental in seeing those ideals attained by the entire population; the cherry trees are a symbol of international friendship; the National Bureau of Engraving and Printing is the brick and mortar embodiment of the economy; and the United States Holocaust Memorial Museum is a reminder of the consequences of abandoning those values.

HISTORIC MONUMENTS

The imposing **Martin Luther King, Jr Memorial** ❶ (1964 Independence Avenue SW; www.nps.gov/mlkm) honors Dr King and his universal message of a non-violent philosophy striving for freedom, equality, and justice. He is the first African American honored with a memorial on the National Mall and the fourth non-president to be remembered in such a way. It shows Dr King emerging from a mountain and was inspired by a line from his 1963 'I Have a Dream' speech, 'With this faith, we will be able

The FDR Memorial   The Tidal Basin

to hew out of the mountain of despair a stone of hope'. The 30ft (9-meter) -high statue was carved by Lei Yixyin of China.

The many entrances and approaches to the monument represent the openness of democracy, while the gap in the 'mountain' from which Dr King emerges symbolizes victory borne from disappointment. The scrape marks in the stone are reminders of the struggle for freedom and equality. Quotes from King's letters and speeches are engraved on the walls.

When the **Franklin Delano Roosevelt Memorial** ❷ (www.nps.gov/frde) was dedicated in 1997, there already was a memorial to him in Washington: a modest stone slab in front of the National Archives. It reflected Roosevelt's wish that any memorial to him be simple, in front of the Archives, and no larger than his desk. This memorial is much grander. A meandering pathway leads past waterfalls, sculptures, and quotes carved into the granite walls through four open-air rooms which represent each of his presidential terms of office. One statue shows FDR sitting in a wheelchair that he used after the polio attack that paralyzed his legs in 1921. The original plans did not include this sculpture, but leaders of the disabled community argued that showing FDR's disability would increase awareness and inspire others who struggle.

Room One shows a bas-relief of the first inauguration, when the country was reeling from the Great Depression. Room Two has a powerful sculpture, *The Breadline*, which shows demoralized men waiting for charity. *The Fireside Chat* depicts Roosevelt's weekly address to inspire hope. In Room Three, a waterfall symbolic of the chaos and violence of World War II crashes over scattered boulders. In the midst of this, Roosevelt is shown sitting quietly with his beloved dog, Fala, at his side, a reassuring and dependable presence in a time of confusion and fear. The centerpiece of Room Four is a monumental bas-relief representing the nation in mourning

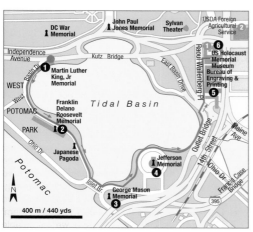

The Jefferson Memorial

Roosevelt's death. Nearby, a statue of Eleanor Roosevelt honors her contributions as first lady and as one of the early delegates representing the United States at the newly formed United Nations.

Tucked away in a grove just past the bridge crossing the Tidal Basin is the **George Mason Memorial ❸** (www.nps.gov/nama/planyourvisit/George-mason-memorial.htm), a small tribute to one of the most important, but least remembered, early patriots. George Mason sits cross-legged on a bench, his tricornered hat beside him, his pose inviting company and conversation.

Mason penned the Virginia Declaration of Rights in early 1776. It served as an inspiration to Thomas Jefferson a few months later when he was tasked with writing the Declaration of Independence. In fact, some of Mason's lines show up in Jefferson's work almost verbatim. But perhaps even more importantly, Mason refused to sign the Constitution in 1789 because he felt it ignored basic freedoms. That resulted in the Bill of Rights, the foundation for American freedoms.

Located on beautifully landscaped grounds, the **Jefferson Memorial ❹** (www.nps.gov/thje) was inspired by the Roman Pantheon, an architectural design that Jefferson liked and used at his home, Monticello. A portico at the top of the building shows the five members of the drafting committee for the Declaration of Independence presenting their report to the Continental Congress. Inside, the bronze statue of Jefferson stands in the middle of the room, holding a copy of the declaration in his left hand. The walls surrounding him are inscribed with quotes about law, the Constitution, the evils of slavery, religious freedom, and education.

Continue on the path along the Tidal Basin to the intersection at Maine Avenue SW and 15th Street NW (the Tidal Basin paddleboat dock is just to your left). It is congested, but there is a pedestrian crosswalk. Cross to 15th Street and continue north to the **National Bureau of Engraving and Printing ❺** (14th and C Street SW; www.moneyfactory.gov; Mon–Fri Sept–Mar 9am–2pm, Apr–Aug 9am–6pm; tours every 15 minutes). The 40-minute tour of the agency is fun for adults and

Cherry blossom

The iconic Japanese cherry trees that border the lake were a gift from Japan in 1912. Their care was originally entrusted to a ladies' garden group. They took their responsibility so seriously that when plans were made to cut the trees down for construction of the Jefferson Memorial, they chained themselves to the trees until the plans were changed. Today, the trees are cared for by the National Park Service.

The annual Cherry Blossom Festival takes places in first week of April, with a parade, lantern lighting, kite-flying, and sushi and sake tastings.

United States Holocaust Memorial Museum exhibit

kids alike. Watch from the gallery as millions of dollars are printed and driven away on huge pallets.

THE HOLOCAUST MUSEUM

The **United States Holocaust Memorial Museum** ❻ (100 Raoul Wallenberg Place, SW; www.ushmm.org; daily 10am–5.30pm, later in summer; free timed tickets, available online up to four months in advance, required Mar–Aug) is a self-guiding experience; there are no guided tours of the museum. Upon entering, visitors receive ID cards relating to individuals who lived in Europe during the Holocaust and detailing their experiences. A reproduction of the infamous arch at the entrance to Auschwitz, which reads 'Arbeit Mach Frei' ('work makes freedom'), forms the entrance to a three-story chronology of the Holocaust. The exhibit uses artifacts, photos, film footage, and eyewitness testimonies of survivors to trace the history of the growth and implementation of the Holocaust. It explores the tools of a totalitarian state to control society and promote persecution. The second floor focuses on the creation and use of concentration camps where millions – not just Jews, but Gypsies, Soviet prisoners, political prisoners, disabled people, homosexuals, Jehovah's Witnesses, and others – were starved, gassed, beaten to death, or died of disease. The upper level addresses those who hid the victims of Nazi persecution, the liberation of the camps, and the postwar efforts to bring the perpetrators to justice.

The permanent exhibit is blunt in its depiction of the Holocaust and is not recommended for children under 11. Particularly graphic materials are behind privacy barriers so parents can decide whether their children should see them. For children between 8 and 11, Remember the Children: Daniel's Story is an interactive exhibition which presents the Holocaust through the eyes of a young Jewish boy. This is not a place for very young children.

The **Museum Café**, see ❶, serves breakfast and lunch. The USDA Headquarters at 1200 Independence Avenue welcomes visitors to its **cafeteria** for the breakfast and lunch buffet, see ❷.

Food and Drink

❶ MUSEUM CAFÉ
United States Holocaust Memorial Museum; www.ushmm.org; $
Across the plaza from the museum building, this cafeteria-style café serves breakfast, salads, sandwiches, and, of course, chicken soup. There are vegetarian and Kosher items.

❷ USDA SOUTH BUILDING CAFETERIA
1200 Independence Avenue NW; $
A utilitarian cafeteria that's primarily for the staff, but open to the public. There's a rotating menu of hot items and made-to-order sandwiches.

The Smithsonian Castle

NATIONAL MALL – NORTH SIDE

Several of the city's most important museums are located here. The Air and Space Museum; the National Museum of African Art; the Freer/Sackler Galleries; and the National Museum of the American Indian display cultures, ideas, and imagination.

DISTANCE: 1 mile (1.6km)
TIME: To visit everything on this tour you would need several days. The best approach is to pick one or two places, then visit one in the morning, have lunch, and tour the second in the afternoon for a comfortable full day.
START: Smithsonian Castle
END: National Museum of the American Indian
POINTS TO NOTE: The nearest Metro stations are Smithsonian (Blue and Orange lines); L'Enfant Plaza (Blue, Green, Orange, and Yellow lines). Alternatively, take the DC Circulator bus National Mall Route (red line). In general, mid-week and mid-afternoon sees fewer crowds. You will be walking far more than you think, so pace yourself. Free Wi-Fi is available at all Smithsonian museums (SI-VISITOR).

Many visitors have little knowledge of the cultures of Asia, Africa, or the American Indian and spending time in these galleries and museums gives an insight into the thinking and beliefs of peoples here and in other lands. Even the Air and Space Museum fits into this definition, for the dream of flight-inspired inventions that changed the way the world travels, trades, communicates, and even, sadly, wages war.

Built in 1855, the **Smithsonian Castle** ❶ (www.si.edu; 8.30am–5pm; free) was the Smithsonian's first building. Once the home of Joseph Henry, the Smithsonian's first secretary and his family, it is now an administrative and orientation center and a good place to plan your day with the help of docents. It contains the crypt of James Smithson, whose bequest created the institution that bears his name. You can grab a cup of coffee and pastry at the café, see ❶, before you start out.

THE FREER|SACKLER GALLERIES

The **Freer Gallery of Art** and the **Arthur M. Sackler Gallery** ❷ (www.freersackler.si.edu; daily 10am–5.30pm; free; see website for details of themed guided tours and after hours events; family activity packs and iPads availa-

Japanese prints, Sackler Gallery   *Folding screen painting at the Freer Gallery*

ble), both of which focus on Asian art, are often referred to as the Freer I Sackler Galleries. Opened in 1923, the Freer Gallery was the Smithsonian's first art museum. Industrialist and art collector Charles Lang Freer donated his personal collection of 9,000 pieces of Asian art, as well as his collection of etchings and works by his friend, James McNeil Whistler. The collection has grown to over 27,000 pieces of art, including ornamental objects from the Ming and Quing Dynasties, jades and lacquerware from 3500 BC, and Japanese calligraphy. The highlight of the Whistler works is The Peacock Room, Whistler's only existing interior design. It was commissioned by an English shipping tycoon to show off his collection of Chinese porcelains. Every surface from the walls to the ceiling is covered with paintings of peacocks. Freer bought the room and its contents and had it shipped to his home in Detroit before donating it to the Smithsonian.

The Sackler Gallery is connected to the Freer via an underground passage. When Dr Arthur Sackler donated his collection of Asian artifacts to the Smithsonian, there was no place to display them and no room on the Mall to erect a new building so the answer was to construct the gallery underground. The Gallery has hundreds of ritual bronze and jade objects, many dating from 3000 BC. Some of the more interesting displays are of pieces from Turkey and Iran and the cultures along the fabled Silk Road.

Adjacent lies the **Enid A. Haupt Garden ❸**. Its plantings rotate seasonally, with an Asian-influenced garden near the Sackler Museum and a Moorish-inspired garden near the National Museum of African Art.

NATIONAL MUSEUM OF AFRICAN ART

The **National Museum of African Art ❹** (950 Independence Avenue; www.africa.si.edu; daily, 10am–5.30pm; docent-led tours on a variety of subjects, see website for details) is the first in the US to make contemporary African Art its primary focus. In addition to a collection of over 10,000 traditional objects, such as ceremonial

Hirshhorn Museum and Sculpture Garden

masks, medicinal items, and divination tools, it has around 1,000 contemporary pieces. The museum offers a multifaceted view of Africa's artistic traditions with innovative, cutting-edge performances and exhibitions.

One of the most visited art museums in the US, the **Hirshhorn Museum and Sculpture Garden** ❺ (https://hirshhorn.si.edu; daily 10am 5.30pm; garden 7.30am–dusk; docent-led tours of museum daily 12.30pm and 3.30pm, see schedule for details of storytimes for children up to 6 years) is a leading voice in contemporary art and culture. Its holdings encompass one of the most important collections of post-war American and European art.

Joseph Hirshhorn, a Latvian-born, self-made millionaire donated his collection of 4,000 paintings and 2,000 sculptures to the country that served him so well. The collection is twice as large as that of the Museum of Modern Art in New York. Paintings by Edward Hopper, Georgia O'Keefe, Mark Rothko, and Andy Warhol are some of the highlights of the museum. Sculpted pieces by Auguste Rodin, Henri Matisse, Pablo Picasso, and Alexander Calder are in the museum or displayed in the sunken sculpture garden outside.

The museum building itself is a piece of art and one of the most recognizable and unusual in Washington. The hollow-centered, drum-shaped gallery hovers above a broad plaza and the 4 acres (2 hectares) of landscaped grounds of the sculpture garden. Architect Gordon Bunshaft envisioned this as a 'large piece of functional sculpture', with curved galleries to expand the visitor's view of works. An entire wall of windows opens the interior to the outside with natural light and a view of the museum's fountain.

The outdoor **Dolcezza Café**, see ❷, makes for a nice snack break.

NATIONAL AIR AND SPACE MUSEUM

On arriving at the **National Air and Space Museum** ❻ (http://airandspace.si.edu; daily 10am–5.30pm, later during high season; tours daily 10.30am and 1pm; free) head straight to the Southwest Airlines Welcome Center. Here you can collect maps, join tours, get directions to specific displays, and find out about special programs. Ask about storytime for younger kids. The free app, Go Flight, includes an interactive map, the option to design a personalized tour, details about artifacts, and highlights of the museum presented in Klingon.

There are 23 galleries covering every imaginable aspect of flight, from the golden age of barnstormers through World War I, World War II, Sea-Air Operations, and jet aviation. Aeronautical science exhibits explain how things fly and how navigation works, and cover the race to the moon, exploration of our solar system, and the galaxy beyond.

The Boeing Milestones of Flight Hall is crammed with famous aircraft,

National Air and Space Museum

including *The Spirit of St Louis*, the *Bell X-1*, which first broke the sound barrier, the Mercury *Friendship 7* capsule flown by John Glenn, Mariner, Pioneer, and Viking planetary explorers, and the Star-ship *Enterprise* (or at least the model used in the original TV series.)

Throughout the museum, Discovery Stations staffed by volunteers encourage learning through hands-on activities related to aviation, space exploration, astronomy, and geology. The Public Observatory (Wed–Sun noon–3pm, weather permitting, see website for details of nighttime events) lets you look at sunspots (with safe solar filters), Venus, and other stellar wonders. Science demonstrations are presented throughout the museum every day in different galleries.

The IMAX Theater (extra charge) shows themed movies during the day and current blockbusters at night. The Einstein Planetarium has free shows at 10.30am, but enquire at the Welcome Desk as tickets may be needed. Hugely popular, although not free, are the Virtual Reality, Interactive Mission, and Capsule Simulators. The VR experience sends you on a spacewalk mission around the International Space Station. Interactive flight simulators let you 'fly' sorties in classic fighters like the P-51 Mustang, F-4 Phantom, and F-16 Falcon. The simulator rides offer a choice of adventures. You can fly with the Red Baron, participate in an orbital mission and re-entry, or be a passenger in planes from all generations of flight.

The **Wright Place Food Court**, see ❸, has a full complement of fast food outlets.

NATIONAL MUSEUM OF THE AMERICAN INDIAN

The distinctive curved shape of the **National Museum of the American Indian ❼** (www.nmai.si.edu; daily 10am–5.30pm; audio tours available for download; free) is the first indication that you are entering a place where Western concepts of logic and living do not always apply. The building reflects the native philosophy of the world as a circle of life and understanding. The forests, wetland, meadows, and mountains essential to the life and beliefs of American Indians are represented in a landscaping scheme that covers much of the site. Notice the 40 'grandfather rocks', quarried in Quebec and blessed by the Montagnais First Nations of Quebec to remind visitors of the native people's relationship to the earth and their endurance in the face of adversity. The structure lines up almost exactly to the dome of the Capitol, the site of political maneuvering that saw over 300 treaties written and then broken, lands taken, and cultures eradicated.

The centerpiece of the museum's interior is the Potomac rotunda, named after the tribe that once occupied the land that is now Washington, DC. Its inspiration is the tribal circles used by native nations for council meetings, celebrations, and layout of camps. Fashioned from red granite and adorned with motifs that

The National Museum of the American Indian

relate to the solstice and equinox, it is a staging area for performances of plays, native dance, and craft demonstrations.

Food and Drink

① CASTLE CAFÉ
Smithsonian Castle; $
This self-serve restaurant is convenient for visitors to the Information Center. It opens 90 minutes before the museums and galleries with breakfast items, and sells antipasti, organic salads, sandwiches, and soups, plus espresso and cappuccino. Free Wi-Fi.

② DOLCEZZA CAFÉ
Hirshhorn Museum; $
At this seasonal pop-up café in the sculpture garden, you can enjoy coffee, pastry, and gelato in the art-filled plaza. Free Wi-Fi.

③ THE WRIGHT PLACE FOOD COURT
National Air and Space Museum; $
This is a large, commercial food court, with McDonalds, Boston Market, and Donatos Pizzeria staying very busy.

④ MITSITAM NATIVE FOODS CAFÉ
National Museum of the American Indian; $
'Mitsitam' means 'let's eat' in the Delaware and Piscataway language. The menu offers indigenous cuisines from throughout the Western Hemisphere. Service is cafeteria-style, but the seating is more intimate and overlooks the grounds.

Exhibits attempt to advance knowledge and understanding of native cultures of the Western hemisphere. 'Our Universe: Traditional Knowledge Shapes Our World' focuses on the world views and belief systems of indigenous people. It features eight native communities in Canada, the US, and Central and South America, and explores how they express the wisdom of their ancestors in celebration, language, art, spirituality, and daily life. 'Many Hands, Many Voices' shows the breadth and diversity of native objects in the museum's collections. 'Americans' highlights ways in which American Indians are part of the nation's identity through advertising, team mascots, street and place names, vehicles, depictions in movies, and folklore. 'Nation to Nation: Treaties Between the United States and American Indian Nations' looks at the history and legacy of the record of broken treaties that lies at the heart of the relationship between Indian nations and the US. It introduces the articulate diplomats of the native tribe as they worked to secure the political, cultural, geographic, and economic future for their peoples from colonial times to the present.

The Kids imagiNATIONS hands-on activity center lets kids weave a basket, walk on snowshoes, or learn how to build a tipi. See website for details of storytelling, artists, and participatory programs.

The **Mitsitam Café** in the museum, see ④, serves meals that reflect the foodways of different regions.

The expansive atrium at the National Gallery of Art

NATIONAL MALL – SOUTH SIDE

Taking in the National Archives, National Gallery of Art, museums of Natural and American History, and the Museum of African American History and Culture, this walk showcase the ingenuity and art of human beings and nature.

DISTANCE: 1 mile (1.6km)
TIME: A full day.
START: National Gallery of Art
END: National Museum of African American History and Culture
POINTS TO NOTE: The nearest Metro stations are Archives Navy Memorial-Penn Quarter (Green and Yellow lines); alternatively, take the DC Circulator bus National Mall Route (red route). In general, midweek and mid-afternoon sees fewer crowds. The National Archives and Museum of African American History and Culture are important for children, but they will probably have more fun at the Natural History and American History museums. To tour everything along the Mall, you would need several days, so pick one or two places that entice you – either from this tour or the National Mall – North Side tour (see page 50). Visit one in the morning, have lunch, and tour the second in the afternoon for a comfortable full day. Free Wi-Fi is available at all Smithsonian museums (SI-VISITOR).

This walk is about turning ideas into reality. The National Archives holds the documents that form the basis of the American experiment in democracy. The national museums of American History and African American History and Culture demonstrate the efforts to realize those ideals in society. The National Gallery of Art, while not 'American', shows how the ideal of self-expression is universally realized in the arts.

THE NATIONAL GALLERY OF ART

The **National Gallery of Art ❶** (6th Street NW and Constitution Avenue NW; www.nga.gov; Mon–Sat 10am–5pm, Sun 11am–6pm; docent-led, accessible, and foreign-language tours available, see website for details or to download a free app for kids; free) consists of two very different buildings. The older west wing is a classical design with a dome similar to the Jefferson Memorial (which was designed by the same architect, John Russell Pope). The East Building is a modern, geometric design by I.M. Pei, which holds most of the modern and contemporary collection.

National Gallery of Art

The **Cascade Café**, see ❶, and the **Garden Café**, see ❷, are good places to stop for lunch, as is the **Pavilion Café** in the Sculpture Garden, see ❸.

Industrialist and Secretary of the Treasury Andrew Mellon built up a collection of 121 Old Masters with the intention of giving it away. It forms the foundation of the National Gallery, which is owned and run by the federal government and not the Smithsonian. Following Mellon's lead, nearly 1,500 donors have shared their treasures with the world through the Gallery.

The gallery chronicles the evolution of Western art from the late Middle Ages to the early 20th century. The most recognizable works by the great 'names' are here: Van Eyck, da Vinci, Dürer, Raphael, and El Greco, to name a few. There are sculptures by Bernini, the charming Degas statue *Little Dancer Aged Fourteen*, a mobile by Calder, and paintings by Jackson Pollock. Americans like Winslow Homer and John Singleton Copley hold places of honor in the American galleries.

The East Building has five floors of European and American masters of the 20th century: Wasily Kandinsky, Picasso, Joan Miro. Pei's design, originally criticized for its large open areas and 'wasted space' is now considered a brilliant concept with its open balconies and bridges sweeping across the atrium giving a sense of openness.

Outside, cross 7th Street NW to the **Sculpture Garden ❹**. It is elegant but informal, with rotating selections of works from the Gallery's collection plus loans for special exhibitions. It is a pleasant green space with plantings of American canopy and flowering trees, shrubs, and perennials around a fountain that morphs into an ice skating rink in the winter. From here cross Constitution Avenue at 7th Street.

THE NATIONAL ARCHIVES

There is a sense of awe when you enter the **National Archives ❸** (700 Pennsylvania Avenue NW; www.archives.gov; daily 10am–5.30pm, timed entry reservations available online; guided tours Mon–Fri 9.45am, reservation required) to stand under the soaring domed ceiling of the Rotunda and see the Declaration

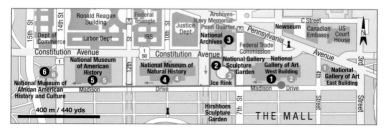

The National Archives   *National Museum of Natural History*

of Independence, Constitution, and Bill of Rights. Up close, they are faded almost to illegibility, although John Hancock's signature is still defiantly large. It is impossible not to feel the weight of the ideals that the documents represent and the ongoing challenges to define and apply them.

The permanent exhibits expand on the import of the documents. 'Record of Rights' starts with an original copy of the Magna Carta then explores how people throughout history have worked to secure their rights. Touchscreens illustrate debates in US history about citizenship, equal opportunity, voting rights, and free speech. The Public Vaults rotate original records and documents from the Archives' holdings. You might see telegrams from Lincoln to his generals or hear audio records from the Oval Office, and study documents of diplomacy and war, legal questions, expansion of the frontier, and national 'firsts'. On leaving the museum, cross over Constitution Avenue and walk a short way down 9th Avenue.

THE NATIONAL MUSEUM OF NATURAL HISTORY

The **National Museum of Natural History** ❹ (www.naturalhistory.si.edu; daily 10am–5.30pm, until 7.30pm in high season; guided tours 10.30am and 1.30pm; nominal charge for Butterfly Pavilion, timed tickets required) is always crowded on weekends from mid-March to mid-May, so consider visiting on a weekday. There are two age-specific activity areas. The

Q?rius Science Center is designed for pre-teens and teens, with a series of interactive experiments to explore anthropology, botany, zoology, and mineral sciences. The Q?rius Jr Discovery Room is on the first floor, near the Ocean Hall. The **Atrium Café** and Café Natural, see ❹, serve lunch and snacks.

The museum is a wonderful smorgasbord of the world's wonders and oddities. Perhaps not surprisingly, it is one of the most visited museums in the world. Its holdings contain more than 126 million specimens of plants, fossils, rocks, minerals, meteorites, human remains, and human cultural artifacts. Only a tiny fraction of them are on display.

Browse through the exhibits and displays and marvel at things like a mummified cat, a live coral reef, a reconstruction of Neanderthals, a live insect zoo, and the massive African elephant that greets visitors in the entrance rotunda.

The Gem and Mineral Collection is one of the most important in the world. The Hope Diamond, Star of Asia Sapphire, and hauntingly delicate Dom Pedro Aquamarine share a room. The Live Insect Zoo shows how all manner of the little critters adapt to different environments. For creepy fun, watch the live tarantula feedings every morning and afternoon.

The centerpiece of the Ocean Hall is a 1,500-gallon aquarium with an Indo-Pacific coral reef ecosystem housing some 50 live, colorful specimens. A fascinating rotating 360-degree display suspended from the ceiling explains the

The Star–Spangled Banner at the National Museum of American History

complex aspects of oceans. A 13-minute video takes you on a dive to the ocean floor in a submersible.

THE NATIONAL MUSEUM OF AMERICAN HISTORY

Heading west along the Mall you come to the **National Museum of American History** ❺ (1300 Constitution Avenue NW; www.americanhistory.si.edu; daily 10am−5.30pm; free). The museum owes more to pop culture than to history books. To be sure, the Founding Fathers get their due, but the displays concentrate more on material development, the consumer culture, and the lives of the average American than on noble ideals and important dates.

It's the artifacts that keep you moving from display to display, marveling at the inventions, diversions, memorabilia, and just plain 'stuff' that illustrate the nation's history. The overriding theme is 'American Stories', a mix of artifacts that include a fragment of Plymouth Rock and Apolo Ohno's speed skates from the 2002 Winter Olympics. There are profound items, like the Star Spangled Banner and the Greensboro lunch counter (site of the first sit-in of the Civil Rights Era), alongside Mrs Calvin Coolidge's bright red 'flapper' dress, President Bill Clinton's Saxophone, and a 9ft (2.7-meter) -tall Statue of Liberty made from Lego.

Each floor of the museum is dedicated to a different theme. The first floor features transportation and technology, with an 1831 steam locomotive, *John Bull*, as the centerpiece. The Transportation Hall demonstrates the change from sedentary agrarian communities to today's auto- and plane-centric society. Another area looks at the development of robots in industry and the home and the decidedly non-gadget-filled Julia Child's kitchen.

The highlight of the Second Floor is The Star Spangled Banner. The flag is displayed in a climate-controlled room. An interactive display features a full-sized digital reproduction that allows visitors to learn more about the flag.

The Third Floor considers the US at war. One exhibit shows how advertising was used to move the nation from neutrality and apathy to an enthusiastic war footing in World War I, which leaves one considering the implications of the same techniques used in current times. The Clara Barton Red Cross Ambulance from the Civil War is on display, as is the gunboat *Philadelphia*, the oldest surviving American fighting vessel. Sunk during the Battle of Lake Champlain in 1776, it was recovered in 1935, along with the cannonball that sent her to the bottom. Also on this level, 'The American Presidency: A Glorious Burden' reviews the personal, public, ceremonial, and executive actions of the residents of the White House, including the first ladies. The final area looks at entertainment, sports, and music. There's a huge dollhouse built on the scale of 1in to 1ft (2.5 to 30cm) with 23 rooms and 1,354 examples of furniture, linens, toys, and household items.

National Museum of African American History and Culture

The **Stars and Stripes Café**, see ⑤, serves BBQ, pizza, soups, and salads, while the LeRoy Neiman Jazz Café has New Orleans-inspired lunch options.

THE NATIONAL MUSEUM OF AFRICAN AMERICAN HISTORY AND CULTURE

The Mall's newest addition is the **National Museum of African American History and Culture** ❻ (1400 Constitution Avenue NW; www.nmaahc. si.edu; daily 10am–5.30pm; timed-entry passes, available up to 4 months in advance, are required; same-day tickets available online from 6.30am or in person from 1pm; free).

The copper-colored building gleaming at the western edge of the National Mall is one of the most popular Smithsonian museums. The distinctive shape is inspired by the three-tiered crowns used in Yoruban art from West Africa. The entrance is a welcoming porch of the African Diaspora of the American South and Caribbean. The entire building is wrapped in an ornamental bronze-colored lattice that pays respect to the ironwork crafted by enslaved Africans in the American South. The 37,000 objects in its collection concern family, religion, civil rights, slavery, segregation, and the visual and performing arts.

The building's six levels tell the story of African history. The lowest level, underground, begins with the height of African nations and kingdoms in the 15th and 16th centuries. It chronicles the emergence of trade and political developments with the Europeans and the rapid change from mutual respect to colonization and the development of slavery. As you move from the lower to higher levels, you symbolically experience the centuries of slavery and the long, slow fight for freedom and civil rights. The deep sense of pride, of place and community, and the strength and resilience required to defy segregation and develop strategies to address racism are shown as counters to the forces that sought to deny those rights and dignity. The upper level galleries focus on African American contributions in the arts, military, sports, and community life, and the ongoing evolution of the African American identity.

The importance of items owned by Harriet Tubman, Nat Turner, and Toussaint L'Ouverture is not overlooked, but other relics that reflect personal histories of unknown people have a deeper impact. There's a hand-embroidered feedsack given by a slave mother to her 9-year-old daughter when the child was sold away; feet and wrist manacles; and garments worn by slaves. From the Jim Crow era, there's a segregated railroad car; a footlocker from one of the Tuskegee Airmen; the casket originally used to display and bury 14-year old Emmitt Till, whose racially motivated murder was a catalyst for the Civil Rights Movement. More positive items are Louis Armstrong's trumpet; gymnastic equipment used by Olympian Gabby Doug-

National Museum of African American History and Culture

las; and Barack Obama's presidential campaign office from Falls Church, Virginia. There are also the handcuffs used to arrest African American Harvard University professor Henry Louis Gates in 2009 at his house by police responding to a call reporting a possible break-in. Expect to spend a minimum of two hours here. After touring the exhibits, plan to spend time in the circular Contemplative Court. Sit on a bench in the quiet, shadowed room where a waterfall quietly invites reflection and encourages reflection and contemplation.

The **Sweet Home Café**, see ⑥, serves lunch.

Food and Drink

❶ CASCADE CAFÉ

East Building, National Gallery of Art; $

The Cascade Café serves an ever-changing selection of soups, salads, specialty sandwiches, seasonal entrees, and burgers in a clean, bright food-court setting. The Espresso and Gelato Bar adjacent to the café sells grab-and-go food items and drinks. Another quick-stop spot is the Terrace Café, which has a great view of the Mall and the Calder mobile.

❷ GARDEN CAFÉ

West Building, National Gallery of Art; $

A serene spot for a relaxing lunch or weekend brunch buffet. The full-service restaurant features a seasonal menu, often inspired by current exhibitions.

❸ PAVILION CAFÉ

Sculpture Garden; National Gallery of Art; $

With a panoramic view of the Sculpture Garden, the café has indoor and outdoor seating. The menu is casual, with pizza, sandwiches, salads, and desserts. Beer and wine are also available.

❹ ATRIUM CAFÉ

National Museum of Natural History; $

Most of the menu items at this busy café are of the burger, pizza, and grilled chicken sandwich variety, but an earth-to-table menu serves seasonal salads. Café Natural sells ice cream, coffee, and desserts.

❺ STARS AND STRIPES CAFÉ

Lower Level, Museum of American History; $

It seats 600, so do not expect an intimate meal or conversation. The menu echoes 4th of July cookouts with BBQ, burgers, pizza, soups, and a salad bar. The LeRoy Neiman Jazz Café on the first floor serves New Orleans-inspired dishes, such as gumbo, muffuletta, and po-boys, in a dining area decorated with Neiman's distinctive, colorful artwork.

❻ SWEET HOME CAFÉ

National Museum of African American History and Culture; $

You can expect to stand in line at this huge cafeteria at lunchtime, but it's worth the wait. Food is inspired by African American cuisines across the country: Agricultural South, Creole Coast, North States, and Western Range.

Octagon House

FOGGY BOTTOM

With the stunning State Department Reception Rooms, fun museum at the Department of the Interior, a gallery of Latin American Art, and a chance to sit on Einstein's lap, this often-overlooked area is definitely worth exploring.

DISTANCE: 1.2 miles (2km)
TIME: A busy half-day or a leisurely full day
START: Octagon House
END: Einstein Memorial
POINTS TO NOTE: The nearest Metro is Foggy Bottom-GWU (Blue, Orange, and Silver lines); the DC Circulator bus stops at Georgetown-Union Station (yellow route). None of these sites are on the 'hot list' for most visitors, so you should not encounter long lines. Kids will enjoy the Department of the Interior film and museum, as well as sitting on the statue of Einstein for a photo. Otherwise, they may grow bored quickly. Aside from the cafeteria in the Department of the Interior building, there are no restaurants or coffee shops along this route. Backtrack to E Street NW or Pennsylvania Avenue NW for other dining options.

Home to several government agencies, scientific think tanks, and association headquarters, Foggy Bottom lacks the cachet of the rest of the city. Even the name is a bit off-putting – a holdover from the days when the area was a swamp at the edge of town. Now, some of the most impressive structures and important organizations are based here, including the State Department, Department of the Interior, American Red Cross, and the National Academy of Sciences. George Washington University, the World Bank, and the International Monetary Fund have also staked out parts of the turf.

PRESTIGIOUS ORGANIZATIONS

It may come as a surprise to learn that **Octagon House ❶** (1799 New York Avenue NW; https://architectsfoundation.org; Thu–Sat 1–4pm; self-guiding tour; free) has only six sides, especially when you consider that this is the headquarters of the American Association of Architects. Built in 1801, it was the first building completed in the new 'federal city'. The mission of the museum is to allow visitors to discover what architecture teaches us about the people who created and used the building. This includes the slaves and servants whose

American Red Cross Headquarters

work allowed its wealthy inhabitants to live comfortable lives. Unlike most museums, the Octagon encourages visitors to handle the artifacts on display: lying on a rope bed, using a coal scuttle, and playing whist in the parlor.

Head south on 18th Street NW, then go one block east to 17th Street NW and the **American Red Cross Headquarters** ❷ (430 17th Street NW; tours Wed and Fri 10am and 2pm by reservation only, email: tours@redcross.org). This stately building serves as a memorial to the women who served in civilian capacities during the Civil War, as well as the headquarters of the international relief agency. It holds artifacts and art acquired since the inception of the organization in 1881. Its most notable feature is the three-paneled stained glass Tiffany windows, which show knights heading into battle while ladies of compassion look on. Elsewhere, niches in the walls hold sculptural depictions of 'Faith', 'Hope', and 'Charity'.

Just south of the American Red Cross lies the **Daughters of the American Revolution Museum** ❸ (1776 D Street NW; www. dar.org/museum; Mon–Fri 8.30am–4pm, Sat 9am–5pm; guided tours Mon–Fri 10am–2.30pm, Sat 9am–4.30pm). Membership of the DAR is open to those who can trace their ancestors back to the men

and women who fought for the colonies in the American Revolution. The museum focuses on the material culture and social history of pre-industrial America, with 31 rooms furnished in styles dating from 1690 to 1935.

The **Organization of American States** ❹ (17th Street and Constitution Avenue; www.oas.org; charge for guided tours, by online reservation only) is a forerunner of the United Nations with members from Central and South America. It is now considered largely ceremonial, although members collaborate in drafting analyses of issues.

Around the corner from the OAS building, the **Art Museum of the Americas** ❺ (201 18th Street NW; www.museum. oas.org; Tue–Sun 11am–5pm; free) is largely unknown, even by lifelong residents of the District. More of an intimate gallery than a full-scale art museum, it is the oldest museum of modern and contemporary Latin American and Caribbean art in the US. Many of its works

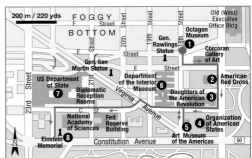

Aztec art at the OAS

Albert Einstein Memorial

have proven instrumental in launching the careers of 'names' in the Southern Hemisphere's art world.

GOVERNMENT BUILDINGS

The **Department of the Interior** ❻ (1849 C Street NW; tel: 202-2008-4743; www.doi.gov; Mon–Fri 8.30am–4.30pm; guided tours of murals 2pm Tue and Thu, reservation by telephone) is sometimes called 'The Department for Everything Else'. It is responsible for protecting areas of environmental concern and historical sites; preserving cultural traditions and welfare of indigenous peoples; protecting wildlife from habitat loss; securing healthy water sources; and providing for the safety and well-being of the public. Many of its responsibilities overlap the Environmental Protection Agency. Displays explain the Department's history, relevance, and current missions, and provide a framework for understanding the interconnectivity among the Department's nine bureaus, as well as the projects in which the Department's 70,000 employees are engaged nationally and internationally.

The **Bison Bistro**, see ❶, is a full-service cafeteria that is open to the public.

The **US Department of State** ❼ (2201 C Street NW; https://reception-tours.state.gov; tel: 202-647-3241; 202-736-4474 (TDD); 45-minute guided tours of the Diplomatic Reception Rooms Mon–Fri 9.30am, 10.30am, and 2.45pm, reservations by telephone at least 90 days in advance) is located in the Harry S. Truman building, three blocks west. In a city filled with impressive galleries and meeting rooms, these rooms seem almost humble. The tour focuses on department's collection of 18th-century American furniture, paintings, and decorative arts. Not suitable for children under 12.

The **Albert Einstein Memorial** ❽ (www.nasonline.org; daily 24hrs; free) is in an elm and holly grove located behind the National Academy of Sciences Building. The bronze statue, 12ft (4 meters) high, features Einstein sprawled on a bench, holding a sheaf of papers which show the mathematical equations of three of his most important scientific contributions – the photoelectric effect, the theory of relativity, and $E=mc^2$. At the statue's base, there is a 28ft (8.5-meter) field of emerald granite, which is embedded with more than 2,700 metal studs. Those represent the planets, sun, moon, stars, and other celestial objects as they were positioned on April 22, 1979, when the memorial was dedicated.

Food and Drink

❶ BISON BISTRO

Department of the Interior Building; $

This is a typical government building cafeteria that primarily serves employees. Because there are no other lunch spots nearby, the menu is better than most such eateries.

GEORGETOWN

Steeped in history and heavy on charm, Georgetown considers itself separate from Washington. There's plenty of shopping, some of the best dining, a beautiful riverfront park, and a glorious gallery, museum, and garden that most residents overlook.

DISTANCE: 2 miles (3km)
TIME: An easy half-day
START/END: M Street NW and Wisconsin Avenue NW
POINTS TO NOTE: Unlike the rest of Washington, Georgetown is not served by the Metro subway system. The best way to reach the area is the DC Circulator bus to Georgetown-Union Station (yellow route). The area can be very crowded on weekends. It's a good idea to make reservations at restaurants, even during the week.

Georgetown predates Washington by at least 40 years. It was a port located at the farthest navigable spot on the Potomac River. It maintained its independence until it was annexed by the District in 1871.

The neighborhood is bounded by the Potomac River, Georgetown University, and several parks that separate it from other communities. The entire area is designated a National Historic Landmark District, due to the concentration of well-preserved colonial and Federal period buildings here. Its history is heavy on important figures. JFK proposed to Jackie at Martin's Tavern, and she lived here following his assassination. Madeleine Albright, John Kerry, and Bob Woodward all call Georgetown home. You'll also find a few embassies here, including those of France, Ukraine, Sweden, and Thailand.

While the vibe along M Street and Wisconsin Avenue NW is invigorating, to find the 'real' Georgetown you should detour down some of the quiet side streets.

M Street NW ❶ is the heart of Georgetown, at least as far as its commercial and tourism industries are concerned. Originally a tobacco warehouse and later stables and a machine shop for Washington's streetcars, 3222 M Street is now the Georgetown Park shopping mall. The western wall overlooks the C&O Canal towpath where there is outdoor plaza seating. **Pinstripes**, see ❶, an Italian-American bistro, is a good refueling stop for lunch and dinner.

As you head south on Wisconsin Avenue NW, you cross the **C&O Canal ❷** (currently drained for repairs), an ambi-

tious transportation scheme that never worked out. Running from Georgetown to Cumberland, Maryland, a distance of 185 miles (298km), it could move goods by barge much faster than wagons. Construction started in 1828, but between engineering and financial troubles, it did not open until 1850, the same day that the B&O Railroad was inaugurated. While it operated in some capacity until 1924, it never made a profit. The entire length of the towpath is a national park, popular with cyclists and hikers.

As you continue down the hill, pop in to **sweetgreen**, see ➋, for a curry bowl or a salad. Eat in or, even better, pick up some ingredients for a picnic at our next stop.

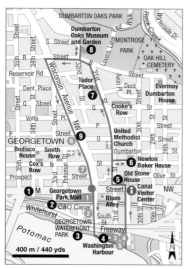

One of Washington's most appreciated public spaces, **Georgetown Waterfront Park** ➌ (www.nps.gov/places/georgetown-waterfront-park; daily 24hrs; free) stretches along the banks of the Potomac River from 31st Street NE to the Key Bridge. The park's centerpiece is the broad flat fountain at the park entrance at Wisconsin Avenue NW. On hot days, kids, pets, and parents refresh themselves in the spray. The River Steps were originally used for spectators watching rowing regattas. Now they are a popular place for picnics and watching the river, birds, and boaters. Notice the 'bio-edge' river bank, which has been turned into a habitat for wildlife. Perhaps the most unusual feature of the park is the Labyrinth at its western edge, which invites quiet meditation as you follow its geometric turns.

Follow the riverfront path eastward to **Washington Harbour** ➍. This architecturally confused complex promotes itself as a destination for entertainment, restaurants, office space, and luxury condominium living. Anchored by a spectacular fountain, its plaza sees outdoor events during the summer. In winter, it is converted into an ice skating rink.

There are many restaurants here. **Bangkok Joe**, see ➌, serves traditional Thai cuisine with American adaptations; **Farmers, Fishers, Bakers**, see ➍, serves farm-to-table meals; and **Fiola Mare**, see ➎, has a justifiably great reputation for fine Italian cuisine.

Go north on Thomas Jefferson Street NW to the **Old Stone House** ➎ (3051

The Old Stone House

M Street NW; www.nps.gov/places/old-stone-house.htm; Wed–Sun noon–5pm; free), a rare example of pre-Revolutionary architecture. Built in 1765, it would have been demolished except for a case of mistaken identity. In 1791, while Washington and Pierre L'Enfant were negotiating with landowners, they stayed in a tavern owned by John Suter. His son, also named John, ran a shop in the Old Stone House. Over time, local lore determined that the tavern and shop were in the same building and the idea that Washington might have stayed there assured its preservation.

From here, go west to 31st Street then turn right. Turn right again and take a stroll along N Street NW. The house at No. 3017 was built in 1794 and owned by Thomas Beall, but is known as the **Newton Baker House** ❻ for the Secretary of War during World War I. After the assassination of John F. Kennedy, Jacqueline Kennedy and her children lived here for about a year.

Return to 31st Street and continue north up the steep hill to **Tudor Place** ❼ (www.tudorplace.org; Tue–Sat 10am–4pm, Sun noon–4pm; guided tours on the hour), a grand residence with an impeccable historic pedigree. It was built in 1816 by a granddaughter of Martha Washington and a son of Georgetown's first mayor. It remained in the family until the death of Armistead Peter III, the founder's great-great-grandson. It opened to the public as a museum in 1988 and is one of the few remaining historic urban estates that retain most of the original landscape. The house has a collection of decorative arts dating from the first years of the estate, including over 100 objects from Mount Vernon.

Just north of Tudor Place, **Dumbarton Oaks** ❽ (www.doaks.org; Tue–Sun 11.30am–5.30pm; architecture tour: 1.30pm second and fourth Sat of the month; museum highlights: Thu–Fri 1pm; no tours in Aug) was purchased in 1920 by Mildred and Robert Woods Bliss as a 'country home in the city'. Bliss, a former ambassador to Argentina, collected Byzantine and pre-Columbian art. His wife dedicated herself to designing 10 acres (4 hectares) of the 53-acre (21-hectare) estate as formal gardens which feature terraced landscaping, 10 pools, nine fountains, and an orangery.

Several famous musicians performed in the lavish Music Room, including Igor Stravinsky. He was commissioned to write the Dumbarton Oaks Concerto for the couple's 40th wedding anniversary. In 1944, representatives from the US, UK, China, and Soviet Union gathered at the house for talks that led to the formation of the United Nations.

The museum's Byzantine collection is comprised of over 1,500 textiles, mosaics, crosses, and other liturgical items. The pre-Columbian collection is housed in glass pavilions so that sunlight envelops the gold jewelry, jade statues, and stone masks.

Leaving Dumbarton House, go west on R Street to **Wisconsin Avenue NW** ❾.

Dumbarton Oaks

Georgetown houses

The stroll down the hill back to M Street passes some of the more interesting shops and upscale boutiques. If you prefer to take the DC Circulator bus back to M Street, there is a bus stop at R Street and Wisconsin Avenue NW.

Boulangerie Christophe, see ⑥, is a corner of France with fresh-baked breads and freshly prepared breakfast and lunch items. **Martin's Tavern**, see ⑦, is a popular place for lunch or dinner with a lot of history.

Food and Drink

① PINSTRIPES

1064 Wisconsin Avenue NW; $$

A bistro with bocce ball? It works. The bistro features Italian specialties served in an open, clean, contemporary space. You can play bocce ball before or after your meal, or dine on the outside terrace that overlooks the C&O Canal towpath.

② SWEETGREEN

1044 Wisconsin Avenue NW; $

With a regionally sourced, seasonal menu, sweetgreen offers healthy eating that is also appetizing. Choose between warm bowls of greens and proteins or salads. An open feel with a few tables, but it's mostly to go.

③ BANGKOK JOE

Washington Harbour; $$

This Thai/Asian-themed restaurant is best known for its Dumpling Bar, which features 20 handcrafted delicacies paired with house made sauces. The bar gives an Asian twist to many familiar cocktails.

④ FARMERS, FISHERS, BAKERS

Washington Harbour; $$

The menu at this upscale restaurant is regionally inspired and made from scratch. Lunches are a good deal with share plates and $9 basic salads. There is a 'Farmers' Market' buffet on weekends.

⑤ FIOLA MARE

Washington Harbour; $$$

One of the most acclaimed restaurants in Washington, it features Mediterranean seafood dishes. A bit pricey a la carte, but the tasting and prix fixe meals are a good deal, as is the Presto! Lunch at the Bar.

⑥ BOULANGERIE CHRISTOPHE

1422 Wisconsin Avenue NW; $

With a courtyard in the back and tables overlooking the street in front, breakfast or lunch here is delightful. The selection of morning pastries and Pain Perdue makes you linger over your coffee.

⑦ MARTIN'S TAVERN

1264 Wisconsin Avenue NW; $$

With wood-paneled walls, booths, and outdoor seating, this mainstay of Georgetown has been around since 1933. There's a reliable menu of comfort foods and steaks.

Union Station

DOWNTOWN EAST

Washington is more than historic, governmental, and commemorative sites. There are plenty of activities to spark the imagination and places to play, shop, and just relax. This walk is particularly inviting for families, with plenty of hands-on fun.

TIME: a full day
START: Union Station
END: Newseum
DISTANCE: 2 miles (3km)
POINTS TO NOTE: The nearest Metro stations are Union (Red line) or Gallery Place/Chinatown (Green, Red, and Yellow lines); the DC Circulator bus stops at Union Station-Navy Yard Metro (blue route), Georgetown-Union Station (yellow route), National Mall (red route). The sites in this area are always popular, although afternoons see somewhat smaller crowds. This is a great walk for kids. Plan to spend a lot of time at the National Building Museum if you have younger children; the Newseum is less interesting for kids. Some of the points of interest on the Downtown West walk (see page 73) are just the other side of 7th Street so you might want to review that before making a final choice of what to see. There is a great deal of road construction along New York Avenue, around New Jersey Avenue, which can require detours along a few side streets.

This walk provides children with a chance to play and parents to relax a bit. The energy in Union Station is invigorating; the displays at the Postal Museum are colorful and interesting; Chinatown gives a sliver of a glimpse into another culture; while the National Building Museum offers kids (and parents) a lot of hands-on diversions.

UNION STATION

Travelers, commuters, shoppers, and tourists surge and flow in perpetual motion at **Union Station ❶** (www.union stationdc.com). The glorious Beaux-Arts temple to transportation was the largest train station in the world when it opened in 1908. With the decline of train travel in the late 20th century, the building fell into disrepair, but in 1981, a coalition of public and private funds financed a rescue job, restoring its grandeur and sense of romance. This is the center point for much of DC's public transportation. There is a Metro stop and several routes of the DC Circulator bus cross here, as well as several Metrobus

The National Postal Museum

lines. Some of the sightseeing bus tours begin and end their journeys here. If you are not familiar with the location of the things you want to see, a bus tour can help to get you oriented. The station is also a glorious shopping mall. The three levels of the building create a vast, upscale shopping experience.

The lower level of the station is a vast **food court**, see ➊, with all of the familiar fast food chains well represented.

NATIONAL POSTAL MUSEUM

Housed in the original Washington Post Office (a branch post office still operates here), the **National Postal Museum** ➋ (2 Massachusetts Avenue NW; www. postalmuseum.si.edu; daily 10am–5.30pm; 45-minute guided tours 11am and 1pm; itineraries and kids' activities can be downloaded from the website; free) has the world's largest philatelic collection. The William Gross Stamp Gallery displays over 20,000 stamps divided by theme. The museum charts America's mail service from the days of the Pony Express and barnstorming early airmail pilots (several planes are on display) to modern high-tech operations. There's also Owney, the taxidermied mutt who spent years riding the rails across country in postal railroad cars and traveled with the mail by steamship to Asia and Europe.

Two fascinating exhibits go behind the scenes to show how involved the movement of mail is. The first traces how the Postal Service evolved from a haphazard attempt to send letters by whoever and whatever was available to its current intricate network of computers, machin-

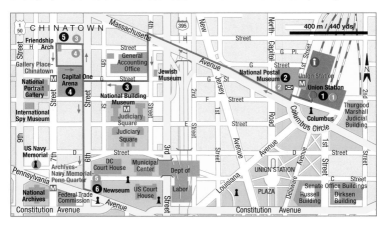

The National Building Museum

ery, digital scanning, and the humans who deliver 700 million pieces of mail to 150 million addresses every day. Another looks at the US Postal Inspection Service, one of the country's oldest federal law enforcement agencies. It protects the mail, post offices, and postal employees and is tasked with restoring postal service after a disaster, disrupting drug trafficking, and combatting mail fraud.

NATIONAL BUILDING MUSEUM

Head northwest up Massachusetts Avenue for about half a mile, then turn left into 6th Street NW. Continue south to the junction with F Street NW – the imposing red building to your right is the **National Building Museum** ❸ (401 F Street NW; www.nbm.org; Mon–Sat 10am–5pm, Sun 11am–5pm; docent-led tours of building 11.30am, 12.30pm, and 1.30pm), which explores architecture, design, engineering, construction, and urban planning.

Originally the offices for distributing pensions to Civil War veterans and their families, the building is less ornate than most others in Washington. Step inside, however, and you are standing in one of the city's most stunning interiors – a massive Great Hall with colossal Corinthian columns and a 1,200ft (366-meter) -long memorial to Civil War veterans. Several presidential inaugural balls have been held here.

Exhibits can be as academic as explaining the art of building in layperson's terms, or as fun as 'Around the World in 80 Paper Models'. The Building Zone (Mon–Sat 10am–4pm, Sun 11am–4pm; 45-minute play sessions) lets 2–6-year-olds play at being contractors and architects, and explore 'green living' in a custom-built playhouse. For older kids, Play, Work, Build introduces the connections between play, design, and the work of architects and engineers. There's a hands-on block play area, and an original digital interactive area that lets kids fill an entire wall with virtual blocks – and then knock them down.

The **Firehook Café**, see ❷, serves breakfast and lunch daily.

The **Capitol One Arena** ❹ (601 F Street NW; www.capitolonearena.monumentalsportsnetwork.com) is the primary venue for professional and collegiate team sports in the District. All of the city's indoor pro teams play here: the Washington Valor indoor football team, NBA Wizards, WNBA Mystics, NHL Capitals, and NCAA's Georgetown Hoyas men's basketball team.

From here, walk north on 6th Street to the Gallery Place passage at the north end of the arena. Go west through the passage, then right onto 7th Street NW.

CHINATOWN

The Friendship Arch at 7th and H streets NW marks the entrance to Washington's **Chinatown** ❺. Its seven roofs rise 60ft (18 meters) above the street and it is decorated with 7,000 tiles and

Chinatown   *9/11 exhibit at the Newseum*

272 hand-painted dragons, promising good luck and safety to all who pass beneath it. It celebrates friendship with Washington's sister city of Beijing and is the largest such single-span archway in the world.

Once home to a sizeable Chinese population, development of the area around the Capitol One Arena saw much of the historic neighborhood torn down. The city constructed the Wah Luck House for mostly elderly residents of the neighborhood who did not have the means or desire to move. The 2010 census indicated only about 3,000 Chinese live within the boundaries of Chinatown, just one-fifth of the population.

There is a Chinese Community Church and several Chinese-American Cultural associations. While there are still shops selling Chinese merchandise, much of it souvenirs for tourists, and the nearest Chinese grocery store is in Virginia.

The most prominent businesses are the Chinese and Asian restaurants, most of which are family-owned. **Tony Cheng's**, see ❸, is known for Mongolian barbecue and a good lunch or dinner stop. For a bizarre mingling of history and culture, **Wok and Roll**, see ❹, is a restaurant and karaoke bar in the Mary Surratt House, used by John Wilkes Booth before he assassinated Abraham Lincoln.

Notice that the outdoor signage of all the stores, including major national retailers, is in Chinese as well as English. That's by city ordinance, to help the community retain its cultural identity.

THE NEWSEUM

From Chinatown, go east on H Street NW, then turn right into 6th Street NW and head south to the **Newseum** ❻ (555 Pennsylvania Avenue NW; www.newseum.org; Mon–Sat 9am–5pm, Sun 10am–5pm; First Amendment Highlights Tour 10am, 11.30am, 1.30pm, and 4pm).

The Newseum promotes, explains, and defends free expression and the five freedoms of the First Amendment: religion, speech, press, assembly, and petition. Since it opened in 2008, more than 7 million people have visited the building, located almost halfway between the Capitol and the White House. There's no figure on how many people have lingered in front of the building, where the front pages of 80 of the day's newspapers are displayed: one from each state, the District, and a sampling of foreign papers.

Seven levels house interactive exhibits in 15 galleries and 15 theaters. There is the broadcast tower from the top of the World Trade Center, eight concrete sections from the Berlin Wall, and the first remote broadcast satellite truck. Budding broadcast journalists are challenged to write, edit, and deliver a breaking news story. The Pulitzer Prize Photographs Gallery features the most comprehensive collection of those photographs ever assembled, plus interviews with many of the photographers.

The Pulitzer Prize Photographs Gallery at the Newseum

Other displays highlight the risks journalists take around the world and a memorial wall lists those who have died covering wars or on other dangerous assignments, or who have been killed in retaliation for their reporting. Not all of the displays are serious. First Dogs takes a look at White House pets, and the displays of political cartoons – while serious in intent – often provoke smiles for their insights.

The Food Section, see ❺, is a small food court with a lunch menu developed by Wolfgang Puck. **The Source**, see ❻, is a fine dining experience with an Asian theme.

Food and drink

❶ FOOD COURT
Lower Level, Union Station; $
It's hard to believe that this crowded, functional space has anything in common with the grand, gleaming architecture on the levels above. All of the major and regional fast food chains are here. Only a few, like Johnny Rockets, offer table service.

❷ FIREHOOK CAFÉ
National Building Museum; $
A satellite of the local bakery, coffeehouse, and light luncheon chain, the Firehook Café is located in the main gallery area. It serves breakfast and lunches midweek, and lunch only through late afternoon on weekends.

❸ TONY CHENG'S
619 H Street NW, Chinatown; $
A long-time favorite for lunch and dinner, with Mongolian barbecue the main attraction. You fill a bowl with stir-fry ingredients and watch as the chef flash-fries it on a vast flat table. Busy, noisy, and fun, with traditional Chinese restaurant decor.

❹ WOK AND ROLL
604 H Street NW, Chinatown; $
A casual spot for lunch and dinner with the usual range of a la carte entrees. The Chef's specials are more inventive, including fried sea bass, quail, and Cantonese roast duck. From this very building, John Wilkes Booth left to assassinate Abraham Lincoln.

❺ THE FOOD SECTION
Concourse Level, Newseum; $
The self-service room is surprisingly small for such a large museum. The offerings include a large selection of hot and cold entrees, grilled and cold sandwiches, salads, and desserts. For a quick snack, ice cream, fries, and coffee, try The Express Bar.

❻ THE SOURCE
575 Pennsylvania Avenue NW; $$$
This is Wolfgang Puck's first fine-dining establishment in Washington. Downstairs, a bar and casual restaurant serves traditional Japanese meals. Upstairs, the menu features contemporary interpretations of Asian dishes and a Sunday brunch. Floor to ceiling windows overlook Pennsylvania Avenue.

The Lone Sailor at the US Navy Memorial

DOWNTOWN WEST

A panoramic view of the city, a dose of history at Ford's Theatre, paying homage to those at sea, a celebration of the faces of the nation, and a chance to be a spy – it's a busy day in downtown Washington.

DISTANCE: 1.2 miles (2km)
TIME: A very full day
START: US Navy Memorial
END: National Museum of Women in the Arts
POINTS TO NOTE: The nearest Metro is Archives-Navy Memorial-Penn Quarter (Green and Yellow lines). Following on from the Downtown East tour (see page 68) this route explores the area west of 7th Street NW. Much of this tour is great for kids. The view from the Post Office Tower, Ford's Theatre, Madame Tussauds, the FBI tour, and the International Spy Museum will keep them entertained. The National Portrait Gallery and the American Art Museum have special activities for kids.

In his design for the city, Pierre L'Enfant incorporated plans for a memorial to the sailors, but not until 1987 was the **US Navy Memorial ❶** (710 Pennsylvania Avenue NW; www.navymemorial. org; daily 9.30am–5pm; free, but donations appreciated) finally dedicated. The Memorial Plaza features a 'Granite Sea' map of the world. Terraced waterfalls, masts with signal flags, and *The Lone Sailor* statue encircle it.

The Naval Heritage Center, located behind the plaza, explores the history and heritage of the men and women of the Navy. Interactive exhibits show life at sea and the technology of the Navy. The Navy Log Room has touch-screen kiosks to register and search for Sea Service members and veterans.

Self-guiding tours of the **FBI Building ❷** (935 Pennsylvania Avenue NW; www. fbi.gov/contact-us/fbi-headquarters; free) must be scheduled in advance via your congressional representative at least four weeks in advance. Foreign nationals should contact their embassy, as the rules change often. The FBI Experience is the dream tour for fans of crime scene TV shows. It features interactive exhibits that explain how the FBI operates and goes behind the scenes to the labs and investigations, covering some of the more notable cases.

For a lunch stop, either head back to the Memorial Plaza for burgers and

The Old Post Office

beer at **bDC**, see ①, or try **Central Michel Richard**, see ②, a convivial bistro across the street from the Old Post Office (see below). **Ollie's Trolley**, see ③, on the corner of 12th and E streets, is a good local fixture for burgers and fries with kitschy antiques.

The **Old Post Office Clock Tower** ❸ (12th Street NW; daily 9am–5pm; free) has had several incarnations since it first opened in 1899. When a larger building opened in 1914 (the site of the Postal Museum, see page 69), this structure housed various government buildings and several failed retail/office centers. In 2012, the building was leased to The Trump Organization for redevelopment and reopened as a luxury hotel in 2016. The National Park Service maintains ownership and control of the Clock Tower, which can be accessed from the courtyard of the Starbucks on 12th Street. It is one of the tallest structures in the city, rising 315ft (96 meters). Its observation deck, 270ft (82 meters) above street level, offers panoramic views of the city and surrounding terrain. On a clear day, you can see the Blue Ridge Mountains to the west. The clock tower houses the Bells of Congress, replicas of the bells in Westminster Abbey, which are sounded every Thursday evening.

FORD'S THEATRE

Head north on 12th Street NW, then turn left onto F Street NW, then right onto 10th Street NW to reach **Ford's Theatre** ❹ (511 10th Street NW; www.fords.org; daily 9am–4.30pm; timed tickets, required for entry, can be booked online; a limited number of same-day tickets are available from 8.30am), a seminal site for the nation's history. The horror of John Wilkes Booth's defiant act to avenge the failure of the Confederate cause and the aftermath of that night have reverberated in the country's psyche for 150 years with no resolution. Learn about Lincoln's life in the White House and his struggles during the Civil War. You also learn about actor John Wilkes Booth, the roots of his hatred toward Lincoln, and the conspiracy to kill Lincoln and other government leaders that night. A self-guiding tour lets you walk through the theater and view the President's Box from the balcony. In spring and summer, a 30-minute play (extra charge) is staged, which tells the story of the assassination through the eyes of the audience in the theater.

The tour continues across the street at the Petersen House, where Lincoln was carried and where he died the next day. The final part of the tour is the Aftermath exhibit. Interactive displays follow Lincoln's funeral train from Washington to his home in Springfield, Illinois and how the crowds reacted each time the train stopped. Another display recounts the 12-day manhunt for Booth and the trial and fate of those convicted of conspiring with him.

Just south of Ford's Theatre, **Lincoln's Waffle Shop**, see ④, makes for a good pitstop.

Ford's Theatre   *Waxwork models of Nancy and Ronald Reagan*

QUIRKY MUSEUMS

The fun of **Madame Tussauds Wax Museum** ❺ (1001 F Street NW; www.madametussauds.com; daily 10am–6pm) has a dark origin. Living at Versailles as an art tutor to the King's sister, she had to prove her loyalty to the French Revolutionaries by making death masks of executed nobles, including the King and Marie Antoinette. She moved to England, taking her gruesome relics with her, and her descendants continued and expanded the display. Washington's museum is understandably skewed toward political and historical personal-

ities – here you'll find all 45 presidents and several First Ladies; historical figures, celebrities, and sports stars. Nearby **Pi Pizzeria**, see ❺, is a good stop for lunch, or a casual dinner, and a beer.

What better place for a spy museum than Washington, DC? The **International Spy Museum** ❻ (800 F Street NW; www.spymuseum.org; Mon–Sat 10am–6pm, Sun 11am–6pm) is the only public museum that explores the craft, practice, history, and role of espionage. While much of the museum is fun, such as the exhibit about James Bond villains, its more serious mission is to provide a global perspective on an all-but-invisible profession that has shaped history and continues to have a significant impact on world events. There are more than 200 spy gadgets and weapons on display, and a 'Secret History of History' that relates the stories of undercover operatives.

ART GALLERIES

The mission of the **National Portrait Gallery** ❼ (8th and F streets NW; www.npg.si.edu; daily 11.30am–7pm; docent-led tours Mon–Fri noon and 2.30pm, Sat–Sun 11.45am, 1.30pm, 3.15pm, and 4.30pm; joint tours of the National

James Bond display at the International Spy Museum

Adams Morgan and Logan Circle

The Adams Morgan neighborhood, just north of DuPont Circle, is one of Washington's most diverse communities. It emerged from a radical community initiative to promote cooperation among racially segregated residents in the mid-1950s. Home to a large Hispanic population, it is also where refugees and newcomers from other lands create their own small enclaves. The center of the neighborhood are the 2300–2400 blocks of 18th Street NW. Restaurants, shops, and nightlife are centered here. Look for the brightly-colored mural of a busty lady at Madam's Organ club and the Toulouse-Lautrec-style mural on 18th Street NW. The neighborhood celebrates every September with a giant block party.

The hottest neighborhood in DC is Logan Circle, just a few blocks east of DuPont Circle. For many years, it was the focus of the city's African American intellectual and social life, but after World War II, the area declined and it became one of DC's more crime-ridden districts. In recent years, things have improved. Attracted by lower rents, budding entrepreneurs are opening businesses that, in turn, are attracting renters and buyers. This is home to some of the best nightlife and several small theatre companies. Most of the activity is along 14th Street NW, south of U Street NW.

Portrait Gallery and the American Art Museum take place weekly; Explore! activities for children aged 18 months–8 years Tue–Sun 11.30am–6pm in English and Spanish) is to tell the story of America by portraying the people who shaped its history and culture. The gallery presents poets and presidents, visionaries and villains, actors and activists whose lives, loves, deeds, and misdeeds constantly shape the nation's character. It houses over 21,000 works of art and is the only museum in the country dedicated to portraiture. The **Courtyard Café**, see 6, makes for a good lunch stop.

The **Smithsonian American Art Museum** 8 (8th and F streets NW; www.americanart.si.edu; daily 11.30am–7pm; highlight tours at 12.30pm and 2pm; see website for details of themed tours and scavenger hunts for kids; free) records nearly 300 years of the American experience and has the largest collection of New Deal art and exceptional examples of contemporary craft. There is also an impressive acquisition of folk and self-taught art, and African American, Asian American, and Latino work. The Renwick Gallery (see page 33) displays contemporary crafts and decorative art.

Head north up 9th Street then head four blocks west to the **National Museum of Women in the Arts** 9 (1250 New York Avenue NW; www.nmwa.org; Mon–Sat 10am–5pm, Sun noon–5pm; 30-minute 'conversations' focus on two works on display, daily 2pm)

Washington National Cathedral

Food and Drink

1 PESCE
2002 P Street NW; $$

An airy seafood bistro, with daily chalkboard specials and a marble bar in back. The chef focuses on high-quality, fresh, simply prepared seafood. It's cozy on the intimate side, but not fussy.

2 PIZZA PARADISO
2003 P Street NW; $

This is the DuPont location for a local chain with great involvement in the community. It offers full table service and a dozen different pizzas, many of them not the usual combos. Enjoy people watching from outdoor tables in good weather.

3 LE PAIN QUOTIDIEN
2000 P Street NW; $

Branches of this popular chain are everywhere. The food is good and healthy (or not; pastries and jams are decadent). The sun-filled corner café also does light lunches and coffees and pastries to go. Outdoor seating.

4 SAKANA JAPANESE RESTAURANT
2026 P Street NW; $

A very small selection of sushi, but that means it is prepared carefully and correctly. Laid back and cozy; you can sit at the counter and watch chefs prepare your food.

5 BAGELS, ETC.
2122 P Street NW; $

A basic bagel shop that's cash only and with limited seating. They open at 6am for commuters and early risers. There's a long list of breakfast sandwiches, plus whitefish and various cream cheese bagels. They also do lunch bagel sandwiches.

6 CAFÉ DELUXE
3228 Wisconsin Avenue NW; $$

This is a family-friendly diner serving American fare and cocktails, as they put it 'fresh classics from scratch'. The menu is familiar family and comfort food, and there is a large children's menu. They do weekend brunch and have café-style outdoor seating.

7 LA PIQUETTE
3714 Macomb Street NW; $$

This is a convivial Gallic-themed bistro with chalkboard menu that features classic French fare and wines. The decor is more English pub than Parisian hideaway, with tin ceiling, wooden floors, and bar stools around raised wooden tables. Weekend brunches are very popular.

8 HERITAGE INDIA
3238 Wisconsin Avenue NW; $$

A classic Indian restaurant, with white tablecloths and burnished braziers, polished wooden floors and warm overhead lighting. The menu is inspired by traditional meals and upgraded street food. The lunch meals are big enough to serve as dinner. Pre-order carryout on line.

Aerial view of Dupont Circle

DUPONT CIRCLE:
A GALLERY STROLL

With more art galleries than any other neighborhood, plus unique, personal shops and some of the best restaurants and night spots in town, DuPont Circle is on the 'must do' list for visitors.

DISTANCE: 2 miles (3km)
START: DuPont Circle
END: Toolbox Pilates Art Studio
POINTS TO NOTE: The nearest Metro Stop is DuPont Circle (Red line) and the DC Circulator bus stops at DuPont Circle-Georgetown-Rosslyn (blue route). Galleries, shops, and attractions stay open from 6–8pm, with special viewing, artist receptions, discounted meals and prices at stores, and other events such as First Friday DuPont (www.first fridaydupont.org). That includes some places that are otherwise only open by appointment. This can be combined easily with the DuPont Circle – Embassy Row tour (see page 78) for a comfortable full day. If you finish in the late afternoon or early evening, you can finish the day with a meal, and then sample some of the DuPont Circle nightlife. The LGBTQ community has a strong, supportive base here (see page 78). This is a particularly nice area if you want to avoid the large hotel chains closer to town (see page 96).

Before the Civil War, DuPont Circle was not an address that anyone wanted. It was home to lower-end businesses, including a slaughterhouse. But during the Gilded Age, it was Washington's undisputed center of wealth, prestige, and both conspicuous and discrete consumption. Residents included Alexander Graham Bell and William Howard Taft before he moved to even better digs – the White House.

While Massachusetts Avenue NW northwest of DuPont Circle is known as 'Embassy Row' for the many foreign embassies and consulates along the boulevard (see page 78), to the southeast, the avenue is known as 'Think Tank Row', for the number of consulting and policy analysis institutes that are based there. The Aspen Institute, the Brookings Institution, and the American Enterprise Institute are just a few of them.

In the 1970s and '80s, DuPont Circle developed as the center of the LGBTQ community in Washington. While the city is now largely accepting of the LGBTQ community, the area is still its unofficial headquarters and the epi-

Renoir's Luncheon of the Boating Party at the Phillips Collection

center of the annual Capital Pride Festival held every July.

The fountain in the center of **DuPont Circle ❶** is a replacement monument to Admiral Samuel Francis DuPont. His family – the DuPonts of Delaware, as in DuPont chemical industries – thought the statue of did not do him justice, so they replaced it with the fountain. It is a popular spot for wedding photos, people watching, and picnicking.

Certainly one of the most unusual venues for art, **DuPont Underground ❷** (19 DuPont Circle; www.dupontunderground. org; open for exhibitions and events, see website for details) is a gallery and performance space in a subterranean tunnel that was once used for DC's trolley system. Abandoned when the streetcars stopped

running decades ago, it's been refurbished as a great place to display emerging artists. But it's not all experimental. In 2017, it hosted the prestigious World Press Photo Exhibition. Their goal is to provide a multi-disciplinary platform for creative exchange, contemporary arts, and an ongoing conversation about the city.

THE PHILLIPS COLLECTION

Opened in 1921, the **Phillips Collection ❸** (1600 21st Street NW; www.phillips collection.org; Tue–Sun 10am–5pm, until 8.30pm Thu, Sun noon–6.30pm; tours of permanent collection Sat noon, Sun 1pm; spotlight tours Tue–Fri noon, Thu also 6pm and 7pm; free app and audio tours; charge on weekends) was the first gallery of modern art in America. Duncan Phillips gathered works by American and French impressionists, including Renoir's *Luncheon of the Boating Party*. He exhibited his collection in specially built galleries at his DuPont Circle home. Over time, more rooms were added until the family moved out in 1930. Since then, two more wings have been added to accommodate works by such well-known artists as Cezanne, Kandinsky, Paul Klee, Georgia O'Keefe,

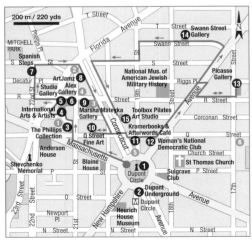

The Spanish Steps

Picasso, and major artists of today like Jacob Lawrence and Anselm Kiefer. Phillips designed the Rothko Room to respect the artist's desire that his works be presented in a small space, so as to saturate the room with color and sensation.

A second permanent installation is a room covered in wax by Wolfgang Laib. The piece, which measures 6ft by 7ft (1.8m by 2.1m) and is illuminated by one bare light bulb, required about 500lb (227kg) of wax. The museum also houses over 1,000 photographs by important American photographic artists.

Tryst at the Phillips, see ❶, serves sandwiches, salads, and coffees for a quick lunch.

CONTEMPORARY ART

International Arts and Artists at Hillyer ❹ (9 Hillyer Court; www.athillyer.org; Mon and Sat noon–5pm, Tue–Fri noon–6pm) is a contemporary gallery focusing on both emerging and established underrepresented artists who have not had a major solo exhibition in the preceding three years.

Studio Gallery ❺ (2108 R Street NW; www.studiogallerydc.com; Wed–Fri 1–6pm, Sat 11–6pm), founded in 1956 by Jennie Lea Knight, is the longest-running artist-owned gallery in DC. It features contemporary art in a wide variety of media by emerging and established artists. Works are displayed in a bright, airy space with great natural light in an elegant townhouse with over 2,300 sq ft (214 sq meters) of exhibition space.

The narrow, cream-colored townhouse accented with russet trim is an inviting stop on the walk. Founded in 1985, the **Alex Gallery** ❻ (2016 R Street NW; www.alexgalleries.com; Tue–Sat 11am–5pm) is a leading commercial art gallery, featuring contemporary American and European painting, sculpture, and works on paper. Artists have exhibited abroad and been sold at international auctions. The Gallery's portfolio also includes works by Picasso, Jackson Pollock, and Norman Rockwell.

From here, head west along R Street and turn right onto 22nd Street.

THE SPANISH STEPS

Built in 1911 at the height of the Beautiful City movement in DC the **Spanish Steps** ❼ (1725 22nd Street NW; daily 24hrs) provide a pedestrian link between Decatur Place and S Street NW. Inspired by the Spanish Steps in Rome, the hillside around the steps is lined with magnolias, cedars, oaks, flower plantings, and flowering trees. The steps have four levels, starting with a wide base at Decatur Place and gradually narrowing as it reaches S Street NW. A small fountain and a granite lion-headed fountain are at the top of the steps. It's a pleasant spot to rest on a warm day.

Go east on S Street NW then turn right onto Connecticut Avenue NW.

Customers browsing at Kramerbooks

You're in the heart of DuPont's Restaurant Row. **Bistrot Du Coin**, see ②, is a delightful Belgian café known for its buckets of mussels. **Sette Osteria**, see ③, is known for its pizza. **Teaism**, see ④, serves light Japanese and Thai-style fare for lunch and dinner.

This area also has some of the city's best shopping. Looped (1732 Connecticut Avenue NW) attracts knitters with its selection of fine and unusual yarns, while Secondi (1702 Connecticut Avenue NW) is nationally known for its consignment of designer fashions from the best labels.

At **Art Jamz** ❽ (1728 Connecticut Avenue NW; www.artjamz.co; Mon–Fri 6–10pm, Sat noon–midnight, Sun noon–8pm) you can access your inner artist at the drop-in studio. For a fee, they supply you with paints, canvas, easel, and smock. The trained staff is on hand to give tips, inspiration, and encouragement. When you finish, you can take your masterpiece with you, or you can leave it and they will recycle the canvas for someone else to use.

During the day, kids aged 2–18 are welcome; after 6pm, it is adults only and alcohol is served, which might loosen inhibitions and encourage creativity.

Art historian Marsha Mateyka opened the **Marsha Mateyka Gallery** ❾ (2012 R Street NW; www.marshamateykagallery.com; by appointment) in 1983. The original wainscoting and trim remain in this classic townhouse, which gives a depth and sense of personality to the works. It is one of the leading galleries of contemporary art, exhibiting painting, sculpture, photography, and works on paper. The gallery's clients include major museums, corporate collections, and private collectors.

Venezuelan-born artist and poet Rafael Gallardo displays his acrylic and paint brush figures and abstracts at **Q Street Fine Art** ❿ (2015 Q Street NW; www.gallardo.net). Granted Permanent Residency in the US as an 'alien of extraordinary abilities' for his visual and written work, he has exhibited in galleries in the US, Spain, and Venezuela.

KRAMERBOOKS

An institution almost since it first opened its doors in 1976, **Kramerbooks** ⓫ (1517 Connecticut Avenue NW; www.kramers.com daily 7.30am–1am, Fri–Sat until 3am) is often crowded. The independent bookstore carries the usual best sellers, but the emphasis is on books with mental nourishment value. The knowledgeable staff is quick to make suggestions, and don't be surprised if that leads to a conversation with another browser. The calendar is filled with author events almost every evening. The late hours in the cozy setting feel like a gift to those who used to read under the covers with a flashlight when they were supposed to be sleeping.

The **Afterwords Café**, see ❺, serves upscale American fare in a lively setting at lower-than-the-DC-average prices.

THE WOMAN'S NATIONAL DEMOCRATIC CLUB

The **Woman's National Democratic Club** ⑫ (1526 New Hampshire Avenue NW; www.thewhittemorehouse. com; Tue–Thu 1–4pm) is a meeting place for Democrats, Progressives, and Independents in Washington. It was originally the home of Sarah Adams Whittemore, an opera singer and descendant of the well-known Adams family of Massachusetts. While it serves as a gathering place for political conversation and planning, the house is also a stunningly beautiful example of the Arts and Crafts style of architecture, with leaded windows and wood panels. The bricks themselves were taken from a rare clay deposit in New Jersey and cannot be reproduced. The signature flowing curves of its high roof are accented by handcrafted copper gutters.

The Club has a small permanent art collection with no particular focus. There's a 17th-century Flemish still life, a c.1700 grandfather clock, and 1894 life-size bronze by Frederick William MacMonnies, the best-known expatriate American sculptor of the Beaux-Arts school. Exhibitions vary between Realism and Impressionism. As might be expected, the small museum focuses on campaign memorabilia, photographs, and political cartoons.

Turn left and northeast up New Hampshire Avenue NW. If you fancy some seafood in a casual setting, detour south to 17th and Q streets to **Hank's Oyster Bar**, see ⑥.

FROM PICASSO TO PILATES

It was almost inevitable that artist Abdi Poozesh would satisfy his love of art by expanding his custom, personally crafted framing services into selling original artwork by different artists. The pieces at **Picasso Gallery** ⑬ (1709 17th Street NW; www.picassogallery. com; Mon–Fri 9.30am–7.30pm, Sat 10am–6pm, Sun noon–5pm) are primarily vibrant, active abstracts which serve as anchors for their setting.

Swann Street Gallery ⑭ (1767 Swann Street NW; www.swannstgallery. com; tel: 202-316-5329 for opening hours) is the exclusive representation of the artistry of Robert E. Kuhn. During his career that lasted more than 60 years, he was one of the very few sculptors who worked in wood and eventually welded steel in the late 1940's. He is considered a master of lyrical, figurative, and abstract sculpture with a wide breadth of subject matter and emotion. The gallery exhibits 100 pieces of Kuhn's art. In addition to his sculptures, there are small and large figurative drawings, acrylic paintings, wood and welded steel figurative and abstract sculptures.

Turn left onto Swann Street NW, then left again onto 19th Street NW to return to Connecticut Avenue NW. There are several nice shops along this block, including The Cheeky Puppy (1709). The pet boutique sells eco-friendly snacks, toys, and pet accessories. Bloom (1719) sells costume jewelry in a bright, mirror-filled store.

Connecticut Avenue seen from Dupont Circle

The **Toolbox Pilates Art Studio** ⑮ (1627 Connecticut Avenue NW; early morning until 8pm) specializes in contemporary drawings, paintings, sculpture, and limited edition prints. Resident consultant Kiril Jeliazkov is a DC-based artist known for his energetic, large-scale abstract explosions of color and movement. He attempts to capture the dynamics of place, people, and spirit as he travels to such locales as Kenya, Italy, Turkey, Spain, and Brazil. As curator at Toolbox, he shows his own works as well as that of other rising artists.

Food and Drink

① TRYST AT THE PHILLIPS
Phillips Collection; $

The light-filled café offers a better-than-average variety of sandwiches and salads, like a ratatouille wrap. There are 'share options' of cheese plates, all-day brunch, and even a classic PBJ (peanut butter and jam sandwich).

② BISTROT DU COIN
1725 Connecticut Avenue NW; $$

'French, Fun, and Friendly'. The staff at this bustling restaurant greets you like an old friend. It's all traditional foods of the countryside, but mussels are the star. Be warned, the full bucket is massive.

③ SETTE OSTERIA
1666 Connecticut Avenue NW; $$

This is a popular Italian café with outdoor seating, perfect for people watching, which is part of the fun of DuPont Circle. The pizzas are baked in a wood-fired oven; heartier fare, like veal scallopine and grilled fish, are served with homemade pastas. There's a nice selection of wines by the glass.

④ TEAISM
2009 R Street NW; $

A nice stop for a quick breakfast before starting your stroll and equally good for a casual lunch or dinner. The atmosphere is one of Zen-like calm, even when it is busy. The menu has many Japanese and Thai items, including bento boxes to go.

⑤ AFTERWORDS CAFÉ
Kramerbooks, 1517 Connecticut Avenue NW; $

Booklovers are not the only people to fill the small dining room in the legendary bookstore. Far from being an afterthought, the restaurant serves a full menu of starters, salads, and a range of house specialties, from fish tacos to hanger steak. Late-night readers can have midnight brunch.

⑥ HANK'S OYSTER BAR
1624 Q Street NW; $$

Perennially near the top of the 'Best' and 'most popular' restaurants in all of DC, it's a New-England-style seafood outpost with clams, an oyster raw bar, and the best lobster rolls outside of Maine. Convivially noisy when it's busy.

DIRECTORY

Hand-picked hotels and restaurants to suit all budgets and tastes, organised by area, plus select nightlife listings, an alphabetical listing of practical information, and an overview of the best books and films to give you a flavor of the city.

ACCOMMODATIONS

There's no shortage of accommodations in Washington. According to tourism figures, there are nearly 32,000 rooms in the city, but, unfortunately, most of them are slightly pricey for the average tourist. Washington has a never-ending flow of visitors, from businesspeople, lobbyists, diplomats, and delegations to tourists, all needing a place to stay. Given that many of them are on generous expense accounts, hoteliers have no reason not to charge all that the market can bear.

Most hotels have generally high standards for bedding, furnishings, and service, but boutique hotels often offer extra amenities such as fitness centers, pools, shuttles, and lounges.

Prices can vary widely, depending on when you are visiting, and drop as much as 25 percent between high and low seasons. However, the popularity of sites like Expedia, Priceline, and Hotels. com mean that you can find very good deals at almost all hotels, even some of the most exclusive. Many hotels now offer packages and encourage potential guests to book directly with the hotel, promising that they will guarantee the best rate. Keep in mind that the quoted price does not include the 14.5 percent room tax or that some hotels charge an additional 'service charge' to cover things like 'free' Wi-Fi, pool, and newspapers.

While many cities fight AirB&B (www.airbnb.com), Washington has embraced it. You can find wonderful prices, locations, and accommodations throughout the city.

> Price for a standard double room for one night, excluding taxes, in high season.
> $$$$ = over $400
> $$$ = $250–400
> $$ = $125–250
> $ = under $125

The Mall and Capitol Hill

Liaison Capitol Hill

415 New Jersey Avenue NW; tel: 202-638-1616/888-513-7445; http://bit.ly/2Bra9Nn; $$$$

Perfectly located just a few steps from Capitol Hill, this boutique hotel offers a modern take on luxury, with clean lines and muted pallets. The seasonal rooftop pool is not to be missed. Very pet-friendly.

Hyatt Place/National Mall

400 E Street SW; tel: 202-803-6110; www.dcnationalmall.place.hyatt.com; $$$$

Guestrooms feature plush beds and state-of-the-art work centers. All have corner sleeper sofas as well as beds.

The Hay–Adams Off The Record Bar

Upper floors have great views of the DC landmarks. The seasonal pool, rooftop bar, and dining are popular in summer. Breakfast is included.

Phoenix Park Hotel

520 N Capitol Street NW; tel: 202-638-6900/855-371-6824; www.phoenixpark hotel.com; $$$$

The rooms are small in this hotel as the building dates from the 1920s, but the staff are warm, beds are lined with Egyptian linens, and just off the lobby is the Dublin Pub. Complimentary coffee and newspapers are on offer every morning.

3rd Street Apartment by Stay Alfred

730 3rd Street NW; tel: 866-232-3864; www.stayalfred.com; $$$

One- and two-bedroom condo suites, less than a mile (1.6km) from the Capitol, make this an attractive choice for families. All suites have full kitchens and sofa beds. There's also a fitness center. It's located near Chinatown and Union Station.

The Jefferson

1200 16th Street NW; tel: 202-448-2300/877-313-9749; www.jeffersondc.com; $$$

Offering as much luxury as the deluxe hotels, but at a slightly lower price, this five-star hotel ranks as one of the top hotels in the country by US News and World Report. There's a 24-hour con-cierge and room service and a spa and fitness center.

Capitol Hill Bed and Breakfast

101 5th Street NE; tel: 202-798-1262; www.capitolhillbnb.com; $

This cozy B&B is in a Victorian brownstone built in 1894 in a quiet neighborhood behind the Capitol. Rooms are small, but comfortable. Several of them share bathrooms. There's a light breakfast each morning in the common kitchen.

Downtown

Hay-Adams

16th and H Street NW; tel: 202-638-6600/800-853-6807; www.hayadams.com; $$$$

Across Lafayette Square from the White House, this five-star hotel is all about luxury and elegance. The ambiance is of an English country home, with fine art, impeccable service, and excellent dining. The 'Off the Record' bar is recognized as one of the world's best hotel bars.

Mayflower Hotel

1127 Connecticut Avenue NW; tel: 202-347-3000/800-228-7696; http://bit.ly/2nk8x5R; $$$$

One of Washington's legendary hotels (for both history and scandals), the Mayflower emanates traditional grandeur with a marble lobby, elegant rooms, and a highly-rated brasserie and equally appreciated wine list.

Trump International Hotel

1100 Pennsylvania Avenue NW; tel: 202-895-1100/866-660-9426; www.trump hotels.com/washington-dc; $$$$

Part of the Trump collection of properties, it's the choice for many people seeking access to the White House. Luxurious rooms are decorated in shades of blue, buff, and gold. Amenities include a spa, bar, and steakhouse.

Willard Intercontinental Hotel

1401 Pennsylvania Avenue NW; tel: 202-628-9100/888-424-6835; http://washington.intercontinental.com; $$$$

This is the grandest of the city's historic hotels. Rooms tastefully combine 19th-century furnishings with modern amenities. The hotel has two restaurants, a bar, and a health club and spa. There are family packages and pets are welcome.

AKA White House

1710 H Street NW; tel: 202-904-2500/888-AKA-0210; www.stayaka.com; $$$

These spacious, contemporary suites offer a high-end getaway. It features an expansive lounge, rooftop terrace, and complete fitness center. The rooftop patio has great views in the summer.

Grand Hyatt

1000 H Street NW; tel: 202-582-1234; washingtondc.grand.hyatt.com; $$$

The modern guestrooms in this large hotel, located in the heart of the city, somehow manage to feel intimate. Guests can access the Metro Center through the hotel lobby. The hotel has both formal and casual restaurants, a fitness center, and shops.

Henley Park Hotel

926 Massachusetts Avenue NW; tel: 202-638-5200/800-222-8474; www.henleypark.com; $$$

This homey hotel in a restored Tudor-style building combines antiques and fine linens with high-speed Internet and a fitness center. It's close to the Convention Center and Capital One Sports Arena. They serve a traditional afternoon tea and the restaurant is known for fine American cuisine.

Comfort Inn Downtown DC

1201 13th Street NW; tel: 202-682-5300; www.dcdowntownhotel.com; $$

A well located hotel with good-sized rooms and amenities like refrigerators, work space, and safes large enough to accommodate a laptop. A free hot breakfast is included in the stay. Family-sized rooms, with rollaway beds and cribs, are available if needed.

Courtyard by Marriott Convention Center

900 F Street NW; tel: 202-638-4600/800-939-3063; http://bit.ly/1br1SW5; $$

This hotel is perfectly located near downtown attractions and a comfortable walk to the Mall. It has an indoor

Swimming pool at the Four Seasons

pool and hot tub. The restaurant features craft beers and casual food and offers a kid's menu.

Hampton Inn Washington Downtown-Convention Center

901 6th Street NW; tel: 202-842-2500; http://bit.ly/1lcDDih; $$

Located close to the Convention Center and near the downtown attractions, basics on offer here include the free hot breakfast, Internet, TV, restaurant, on-site bar, and fitness center. This hotel is particularly accommodating for guests with disabilities.

Renaissance Washington, DC

999 9th Street NW; tel: 202-898-9000; http://bit.ly/1q1L17w; $$

Close to the Convention Center and Sports Arena in Chinatown, this is a good choice for those coming to town for special events. It is also close enough to attractions for sightseeing. There's a state-of-the-art fitness center and a spa.

Washington Plaza

10 Thomas Circle NW; tel: 202-842-1300/800-424-1140; www.washingtonplazahotel.com; $$

Popular with millennials, this hotel is in the Thomas Circle/Logan Circle area (the trendiest neighborhoods for nightlife and restaurants). In summer, there's al fresco dining by the outdoor pool; in winter, a fireplace burns in the lounge.

Hotel Harrington

11th and E Street NW; tel: 202-628-8140/800-424-8532; www.hotel-harrington.com; $

A clean, comfortable hotel that is perfectly located for families. It's close to Chinatown, the Spy Museum and Ford's Theater. The restaurants are among the most kid-friendly in town.

Foggy Bottom and Georgetown

Four Seasons

2800 Pennsylvania Avenue NW; tel: 202-342-0444/00-332-3442; www.fourseasons.com/washington; $$$$

Dedicated to comfort and service, the hotel boasts elegant rooms augmented by an indoor pool, wine bar, and steak house. Family options include babysitting service. There's a hotel car service and multilingual staff.

Georgetown Inn

1310 Wisconsin Avenue NW; tel: 202-333-8900/866-971-6618; www.georgetowninn.com; $$$

A European style hotel that offers charm and luxury. The large rooms have a lot of natural light and great city views. The hotel restaurant features American cuisine. A fitness club, valet parking, and concierge services are included.

Ritz-Carlton

3100 South Street NW; tel: 202-912-4100; http://bit.ly/2BzXR6d; $$$

DuPont Circle Hotel suite balcony

Extreme pampering and luxury are available at this hotel, which is located adjacent to the Washington Harbour shopping and entertainment complex. Butlers serve s'mores in the lounge at night. There's also a bistro and spa.

One Washington Circle Hotel

1 Washington Circle NW; tel: 202-872-1680/800-424-9671; www.thecirclehotel.com; $$
Removed from the bustle of the tourist center but still very close to the action, this hotel is family friendly and welcoming to pets. All rooms have contemporary decor, well-stocked kitchens, and entertainment centers. Walk-out balconies are available.

Georgetown University Hotel and Conference Center

3800 Reservoir Road NW; tel: 202-687-3200; www.acc-guhotelandconference center.com; $$
Located on the campus of Georgetown University, the rooms are well-appointed, but not luxurious, with work and sitting areas, high-speed Internet, and HD TV. It has a strong commitment to eco-friendly practices and amenities.

State Plaza Hotel

2117 E Street NW; tel: 202-861-8200; www.stateplaza.com; $
Newly renovated and conveniently located in Foggy Bottom, close to the West End, it is a bit quieter here than staying in the tourist areas. Many packages are available.

DuPont Circle

DuPont Circle Hotel

1500 New Hampshire Avenue NW; tel: 202-483-6000; http://bit.ly/1PGaH0B; $$$$
The hotel's rooms are stylish and very comfortable, with clean lines and plenty of space. Private suites with balconies overlooking the city are available on the top floor. The brasserie-style restaurant is highly recommended.

Embassy Row Hotel

2015 Massachusetts Avenue NW; tel: 202-265-1600/800-893-1011; http://bit.ly/2hrFAhp; $$$$
A lifestyle hotel for the hip crowd. In an unbeatable location adjacent to the Metro and along Embassy Row, it boasts a rooftop pool, city views, and a trendy kitchen. LGBTQ-welcoming.

Kimpton Rouge

1315 16th Street NW; tel: 202-232-8000/800-738-1202; www.rougehotel.com; $$$$
A fabulous, trendy place with some of the largest rooms in DC. The lively lounge is decorated with leather and animal prints. Suites have kitchens and bunk beds, ideally suited to families.

Churchill Hotel

1914 Connecticut Avenue NW; tel: 202-797-2000/800-424-2464;

A room at the Kimpton Rouge

www.thechurchillhotel.com; $$$
This Beaux Arts building is part of the Historic Hotels of America group and part of the National Trust for Historic Preservation. Standard rooms are a bit snug, but have comfortable beds and nice amenities.

Kalorama Guest House

2700 Cathedral Avenue NW; tel: 202-588-8188/202-297-4999; www.kaloramaguesthouse.com; $$
Four Victorian townhouses turned into a very cozy European-style pension. It's two blocks from the Woodley Park/Zoo Metro. Children must be over six years old to stay. Some rooms share baths. TVs are in the parlor.

Kimpton Madera

1310 New Hampshire Avenue NW; tel: 202-296-7600/800-430-1202; www.hotelmadera.com; $$
Located in the heart of DuPont Circle on a quiet, tree-lined street, it's an oasis after a day of touring. Warm, restful colors and a handmade batik body pillow give the rooms a zen-like feel. Many rooms have city views.

The Baron Hotel

1523 22nd Street NW; tel: 202-293-1888; www.thebaronhotel.com; $
An older property with somewhat dated furnishings, but it is clean and the staff is friendly and helpful. It's just two blocks from the circle and Metro. The Bier Baron Tavern is one of the top beer bars in the country, with over 600 beers.

Southwest Waterfront

Intercontinental, The Wharf

801 Wharf Street SW; tel: 877-424-2449; www.wharfintercontinentaldc.com; $$$$
The first of the hotels to open in the grand waterfront development, it's all gleaming gold and silver in the lobby with river views in the rooms. A fitness center, upscale restaurant, and rooftop pool bar are available.

Hyatt House/The Wharf

725 Wharf Street SW; tel: 202-554-1234; www.washingtondcthewharf.house.hyatt.com; $$$
This hotel is right in the middle of the rapidly developing Wharf, with residential rooms and suites overlook the Potomac. Hop on a water taxi to Georgetown or stroll three blocks to the National Mall.

RESTAURANTS

Dining out is one of the delights of travel and Washington supplies that pleasure in abundance. The challenge is to decide which restaurants to try. Every neighborhood has its own culinary ambiance. Downtown is the haunt of the power brokers and expense account diners. DuPont Circle and Logan Circle are known for moderately priced international restaurants. Capitol Hill is a hot spot for eating out with a fun focus on American foods. The common ingredient is good food prepared by proud, talented chefs.

Price ranges are based on an average cost of a two-course meal with a glass of wine or beer. High-priced restaurants often have luncheon menus that are similar to the dinner menu, but less expensive.

Capitol Hill

Acqua Al 2
212 7th Street SE; tel: 202-525-4375; www.acquaal2.com; $$$
The original restaurant is in Florence, Italy, where it developed a large local

Price for a two-course meal for one including a glass of wine (or other beverage).
$$$ = over $75
$$ = $50–75
$ = under $50

and international following. This has the same menu and replicates the dining experience of the Piazza della Signoria. Choose from tasting menus of salad, dessert, pasta, or steak.

Joselito Casa de Comidas
600 Pennsylvania Avenue NW; tel: 202-930-6955; www.joselitodc.com; $$
Traditional Spanish cuisine from family recipes is served in this friendly neighborhood restaurant. Everything is served in three sizes: appetizer, entree, and family. There's a five-course tasting menu served family style; a three-course lunch prix fixe, and weekend brunch with a Mimosa, Bellini, and Bloody Mary bar.

Rasika
633 D Street NW; tel: 202-637-1222; www.rasikarestaurant.com; $$
This Modern Indian restaurant encourages guests to choose a variety of appetizers and small plates to share. Unusually, griddle and open barbecue dishes are available as well as the more familiar Tandoori. It offers a pre-theater menu and a tasting menu of four or six courses with optional wine pairings.

Barrel
613 Pennsylvania Avenue SE; tel: 202-543-3622; www.barreldc.com; $
Satisfy your inner Southern gentleman at this cozy Bourbon and whiskey bar.

Aged Duck Bomba Rice at Arroz

The kitchen serves Southern staples like ham 'n' honey butter biscuits and fried chicken, but also Jamaican jerk chicken and crab Rangoon.

Bistro Bis

15 E Street NW; tel: 202-661-2700; www.bistrobis.com; $$$

This gem on Capitol Hill is a quietly classic French bistro that's a tribute to the simple pleasure of a properly executed white table restaurant. The entrees are familiar: beef Bourguignon, bouillabaisse Marseillaise, and steak-frites with red wine shallot butter, and there's an elegant cream of crab soup for local flavor. Desserts are equally classic and delicious.

Bullfeathers

410 1st Street SE; tel: 202-484-0228; www.bullfeathersdc.net; $

Sometimes all you want is a good burger and comfort food, and this place takes care of you. In the shadow of the Capitol, it serves pub and grill food in a friendly eat-at-the-bar setting. The burgers are big and hot; there's fried chicken, fish 'n chips, mac 'n cheese, Reubens, and even grilled cheese with bacon and tomato. Don't forget to try the milkshakes.

Downtown

Acadiana

901 New York Avenue NW; tel: 202-408-8848; www.acadianarestaurant.com; $$$

A sprawling, elegant contemporary eatery that raises classic Cajun-Creole dishes to a heightened level. Chef Jeff Tunks worked in New Orleans for years before moving his love for the Big Easy north. He serves the *rémoulades*, *bisques*, and *étouffes* for which the region is known.

Arroz

901 Massachusetts Avenue NW; tel: 202-869-3300; www.arrozbymic.com; $$$

Chef Mike Isabella explores the melding of cultures on the Iberian Peninsula and Morocco. Try chermoula lamb ribs or Moorish chicken. The setting is clean and contemporary with Moorish accents. *Arroz* means 'rice' in Spanish, and it is used as an ingredient as well as an accompaniment.

Mastro's Steakhouse

600 13th Street NW; tel: 202-347-1500; www.mastrosrestaurants.com; $$$

An upscale restaurant that serves sizzling steaks on 400-degree platters and towering seafood selections brimming with oysters. There's a love of the excess here, like mashed potatoes topped with a whole lobster. The lunch menu is similar to the dinner menu, but less pricey.

Occidental Grill and Seafood

1475 Pennsylvania Avenue NW; tel: 202-783-1475; www.occidentaldc.com; $$$

This is a classic white tablecloth restaurant serving surf and turf and other standards under the watchful gaze of portraits of statesmen on the wall. It's

been the gathering place of notables for over a century, from Churchill to Tom Clancy.

Brasserie Beck

1101 K Street NW; tel: 202-408-1717; www.brasseriebeck.com; $$

Voted one of the Best New Restaurants in America, this is a contemporary European brasserie in the McPherson Square neighborhood. Chef Robert Wiedmaier stays true to his Belgian roots, with moules and frites with a trio of dipping sauces or Beef Carbonnade. The bar boasts the most comprehensive Belgian beer list outside Brussels.

Café du Parc

1401 Pennsylvania Avenue NW; tel: 202-942-7000; www.cafeduparc.com; $$

A contemporary French bistro that creates inventive takes on French cuisine. In good weather, take advantage of the outdoor seating. Evening meals are regional French favorites; try the *petit plats* afternoon menu of mussels, terrines, and roasted chicken. Le Bar pours boutique French wines rarely offered in American restaurants.

Ethiopic

401 H Street NE; tel: 202-675-2066; www.ethiopicrestaurant.com; $$

The restaurant uses traditional ingredients and recipes to give guests a true taste of Ethiopia. The authentic flair continues in the decor, which is simple and modern, but accented with traces of the ancient script of the country's classic language. Newcomers to the cuisine should try the four- or seven-course sampler menu.

701 Restaurant

701 Pennsylvania Avenue NW; tel: 202-393-0701; www.701restaurant.com; $$

The feel is that of a private club, with muted lighting and mocha-toned accents, far removed from the bustle of Pennsylvania Avenue and the Navy Memorial Plaza, which it overlooks. The prices are surprisingly moderate, given the location and the menu. Try the rockfish with gnocchi and Spanish Chorizo, or the house-rolled spaghetti with various sauces. There is also a three course pre-theater menu.

Woodward Table

1426 H Street NW; tel: 202-347-5353; www.woodwardtable.com; $$

The main restaurant serves southern-inspired dishes, like cider-glazed pork, cast iron skillet mussels, and sweetbread and waffles. Happy Hour regulars gather at the 38ft (11.6-meter) bar for drinks. Woodward Takeout Food serves interesting salads, milk shakes, lemon squares, specialty lemonades, and more.

Po' Boy Jim

709 H Street NE; tel: 202-621-7071; www.poboyjim.com; $$

Family owned, this is a comfortable joint where Jimmy Buffet would feel at home. It serves low-country classics

like gumbo and shrimp and grits, wings with an assortment of sauces, and batter fried fish. The Po' Boy sandwiches are also classic: oyster, pulled pork, or andouille sausage.

DuPont Circle

Russia House

1800 Connecticut Avenue NW; tel: 202-234-9433; www.russiahouselounge.com; $$$

A bit of Tsarist Russia near Embassy Row, it's an intimate Russian dining lounge in an ornate four-story townhouse. The menu includes a selection of caviars. On weekends, the upper level becomes 'The Winter Palace' dance venue with live music.

Firefly

1310 New Hampshire Avenue NW; tel: 202-861-1310; www.firefly-dc.com; $$

Salvaged barn wood tables and recycled wine bottle glassware set the rustic setting in this popular local spot. The kitchen does inventive takes on the farm-to-table trend. There's a full gluten-intolerant menu, but it is not a gluten-free kitchen.

Mission

1606 20th Street NW; tel: 202-525-2010; www.missiondupont.com; $$

All of the favorites of Mexican cuisine are produced at a high quality, including 10 different kinds of tacos and margaritas. The weekend brunch includes one entree, endless chips and salsa, and two hours of bottomless margaritas and Bloody Marys.

Zorba's Café

1612 20th Street NW; tel: 202-387-8555; www.zorbascafe.com; $$

Big windows, Aegean blue walls, and a background of bouzouki music set the mood in this neighborhood Greek café. It's family-owned, and the menu is inspired by family recipes: souvlaki wrapped in pita bread and kebabs served with a generous helping of convivial conversation.

Foggy Bottom

Founding Farmers

1924 Pennsylvania Avenue NW; tel: 202-822-8783; www.wearefoundingfarmers.com; $$

This upscale casual, sustainably sourced farm-to-table restaurant has been hugely popular since it opened. It defines its setting as 'urban farmhouse' with clean open spaces and original artwork by local artists on the walls. The menu is simple food done well – Yankee pot roast, handmade pastas, vegetarian risottos, and spinach, bacon, and blue cheese salad.

Notti Blanche

824 New Hampshire Avenue NW; tel: 202-298-8085; www.universityinndc.com; $$

Located in the University Inn on the George Washington University campus, this is a hidden surprise. Terra-cotta-colored walls with classic advertising posters for Italian aperitifs give the place a warm atmosphere. The menu is small, but nicely prepared pastas,

seafood, and chicken are all available. There's a prix-fixe menu that's excellent value.

District Commons

2200 Pennsylvania Avenue NW; tel: 202-587-8277; www.districtcommonsdc.com; $
Anchored by a monumental raw bar and an open-hearth oven for flatbreads, this 'American Tavern' has a menu as diverse as the country. The 'pig board' showcases many styles of ham; there's 'low and slow' roasted duck, and meatloaf. 'Family Meal' time starts at 10pm, a sort of late-night happy hour.

Tonic at Quigley's

2036 G Street NW; tel: 202-296-0211; www.tonicrestaurantdc.com; $
American comfort food with a bit of a modern twist is served in a dining room that looks far more exclusive, with a private club ambience, than the menu would lead you to expect. There's also a nice patio that's protected from the summer sun and showers by a welcome awning. Pan-seared salmon and an excellent vegetarian quinoa-based Cobb salad are served, along with fish tacos, mac 'n cheese, and a curried vegetable bowl.

Georgetown

Iron Gate

1734 N Street NW; tel: 202-524-5202; www.irongaterestaurantdc.com; $$$
This swanky spot with a patio garden and intimate dining room serves Med-iterranean-inspired mezze dishes from their wood-burning hearth and rotisserie. There's a multi-course tasting menu with optional wine pairings from the 400-bottle wine list. Reservations suggested.

Ristorante Piccolo

1068 31st Street NW; tel: 202-342-7414; www.piccolodc.com; $$
It's a romantic Italian trattoria with low lighting, a second-floor balcony, and lovingly prepared rustic dishes. The owner is always on hand, discretely moving among the tables and welcoming guests. Try the hand-rolled porcini stuffed *agnolotti* in a fresh sage and butter sauce. The kids' menu features familiar Italian fare: spaghetti with various sauces and flatbread pizza.

Chaia

3207 Grace Street NW; tel: 202-333-5222; www.chaiadc.com; $
This vegetarian spot demonstrates the relationship between farmers and street food with a 'farm to taco' menu. It serves seasonal, plant-based tacos and sides. Counter service, with a bright, clean, simple dining area.

Mr. Smith's of Georgetown

3205 K Street NW; tel: 202-333-3104; www.mrsmiths.com; $
Just across K Street from Georgetown Waterfront Park, this comfortable neighborhood pub has fed locals and visitors alike for over 50 years. Home-

made pastas, serious burgers, ribs, and fried chicken are all on the menu. Don't miss the sing-along piano set Wednesday to Saturday nights.

Logan Circle

B Too

1324 14th Street NW; tel: 202-627-2800; www.btoo.com; $$

Chef Bart Vandaele transports Belgian cuisine to Logan Circle. The restaurant reflects modern Belgian design, while the open kitchen features charcoal grilling, something unique in DC. The menu has mussels, of course, as well as duck breast, and steak tartare. Belgian waffles are served as a main course or as a dessert with strawberries and ice cream.

Chicken and Whiskey

1738 14th Street; tel: 202-667-2456; www.chickenandwhiskey.com; $$

A 127-year-old row house converted into a neighborhood hangout, which serves Peruvian roast chicken with a 'hidden' whiskey bar in the back (access is through a refrigerator). The chicken is tenderized by a 12-hour brine. The bar serves 99 international and domestic whiskies.

Compass Rose

1346 T Street NW; tel: 202-506-4765; www.compassrosedc.com; $$

Owner Rose Previte draws on her memories of street food, 'quirky' beers, and exotic wines from the 30 countries she's visited for the menu at her restaurant. The food is an international, eclectic choice and is meant to be shared; guests are invited to choose two or three dishes per person. Shrimp with lemongrass from Malaysia; Lamb Kefta from Lebanon; steamed buns from Japan. The back patio has been transformed into a Bedouin tent. Ms Previte also offers a family-style tasting dinner for six to eight people, by reservation.

Le Diplomate

1601 14th Street NW; tel: 202-332-3333; www.lediplomatedc.com; $$

This restaurant pays homage to French café culture. It's a place to savor a morning croissant and coffee or a casual evening with friends. The menu is traditional French – Steak au Poivre, Trout Almondine, Lamb Navarin, veal escalope, and onion soup, all accompanied by a carefully curated wine list.

Southwest Waterfront

Station 4

1101 4th Street SW; tel: 202-488-0987; www.station4dc.com; $$$

This swanky spot serves new American cuisine in the rapidly developing Waterfront district. It's close to the Arena Stage and offers a three-course pretheater menu. Sunday brunches are a nice way to start the week, with a bottomless Mimosa and Bloody Mary bar. Try the Chesapeake Eggs Benedict, which comes with crabmeat on the poached egg.

The patio at Eighteenth Street Lounge

NIGHTLIFE

Fueled by the student population of three major universities and a large millennial presence, Washington's nightlife – while not large – is energetic. The city has a long history of jazz; the DC Jazz Festival, held annually in June, attracts an international roster of artists. Dance clubs are split between those with professional DJs and those with live music. All brag about the quality of their sound systems and size of their dance floors, not to mention the excellence of their bars and specialty cocktails. Intimate lounges for conversation and quieter rendezvous are scattered throughout the District. And there are a few places that showcase performers of other genres, like Americana and indie rock. The Capital Fringe Festival in June brings together avant-garde music, dance, performance, and visual arts. FilmFest D.C., held annually in the spring, screens 10 days of dramas, documentaries, comedies, and experimental movies from nearly 50 countries. Comedy and improv clubs promise a night of laughter, with both national and local talent performing with their off-kilter views on life, love, social issues and – this is Washington, after all – politics.

Dance clubs

Eighteenth Street Lounge
1212 18th Street NW; tel: 202-466-3922; www.eighteenthstreetlounge.com

This is where DC's beautiful people go. With dark red walls, deep couches, low lighting, and antique furniture, it's not what most people expect of a dance club. Each of the three floors has a different theme, so you can find the room that's right for you. Thursday nights features Salsa music.

9:30 Club
815 V Street NW; tel: 202-265-0930; www.930.com

Voted the number one nightclub by *Rolling Stone* and *Billboard* magazines, this is DC's definitive nightclub. It has four bars and boasts one of the largest dance floors in the city. The owners renovated this old building to give perfect views of the stage and great acoustics. The performance schedule is an impressive line-up of solo artists and bands. Tickets can be purchased online in advance.

The Anthem
901 Wharf Street SW; tel: 202-888-0020; www.theanthemdc.com

The same team that owns the 9:30 Club is behind this huge performance venue at The Wharf. It can accommodate up to 6,000 people or as few as 2,500 for shows and concerts, thanks to a flexible staging system. For most shows, you can purchase general admission standing tickets or spring for seats in the theater-style boxes.

Musicians at Blues Alley

U Street Music Hall

1115A U Street NW; tel: 202-588-1889;
www.ustreetmusichall.com

Owned by a DJ and designed to accommodate the needs of guests, this subterranean dance hall has no frills, but there is plenty of room with a capacity of up to 500 people. There is a cork-cushioned dance floor and one the city's best sound systems. The club supports a community foundation, with much of the profits given back into the neighborhood by way of music education programs and grants to non-profit organizations.

Jazz clubs

Blues Alley

1073 Wisconsin Avenue NW; tel: 202-337-4141; www.bluesalley.com

Founded in 1965, this is the nation's oldest jazz supper club. Dizzy Gillespie, Maynard Ferguson, and Grover Washington, Jr. are a few of the names who have performed here. Located in an 18th-century brick carriage house, it has the ambiance of the jazz clubs of the '20s and '30s. The menu is authentic Creole food, which will make you think you are in New Orleans.

Jojo Restaurant and Bar

1518 U Street NW; tel: 202-319-9350;
www.jojodc.com

The U Street corridor was to Washington's black community what Harlem was to New York's. It nurtured a generation of musical talent that is now legendary, and Jojo recreates that

1920's vibe with candlelit tables and an intimate feel. The calendar of artists flows between straight ahead jazz, Latin vibes, and vocalists who perform every Saturday. Sunday jazz brunch jams run until 3pm, followed by New Orleans music night which continues until midnight.

Twins Jazz Club

1344 U Street NW; tel: 202-234-0072;
www.twinsjazz.com

A mainstay of the national as well as local jazz world, this club consistently shows up on lists of 'The Best'. Artists of the stature of Stevie Wonder have appeared here. It's a colorful place, with red walls and a tiled multicolored bar, with a relaxed atmosphere featuring traditional jazz. The menu is a refreshing mix of American, Jamaican, and Ethiopian dishes.

The Hamilton Live

600 14th Street NW; tel: 202-787-1000;
www.thehamiltondc.com

During the day, The Hamilton is an upscale restaurant between the White House and Capitol Hill that serves the business and government community. At night, the 'other' Hamilton opens, a separate performance venue with tiered table seating that surrounds a stage and two large bars. The genre of the shows varies widely: the Eric Byrd Trio, a disco-funk throwdown with Superfly, and the bluegrass and Americana sounds of Scythian.

Pearl Street Warehouse

Other music venues

The New Vegas Lounge

1514 P Street NW; tel: 202-483-3971;
www.newvegasloungedc.com

A landmark for nearly 50 years, this is the place for live Rhythm and Blues. It is open only on Friday and Saturday nights when the world-renowned Out of Town Blues Band takes the stage at 10pm. On the first and third Thursdays of the month, guest bands perform at 8pm.

Pearl Street Warehouse

23 Pearl Street SW; tel: 202-380-9620;
www.pearlstreetwarehouse.com

This is the place to hear any other style of music from all-American folk, rock zydeco, soul, R&B, country, and bluegrass. Here it's all about the music and having a personal experience with the performers. The small, intimate venue allows all seats to be within 25ft (8 meters) of the stage. The very limited menu is all-American classic with a slight ethnic twist; a Cobb salad, vegetable empanadas, and Thai turkey burgers are all on offer. Desserts remain all-American – pumpkin and apple pies and blueberry strudel.

Black Cat

1811 14th Street NW; tel: 202-667-4490;
www.blackcatdc.com

This is a multilevel bar/café with indie, rock, and alternative live music that's been part of the underground music scene since 1993. Most nights, though, it is DJ driven. It's also part of the pinball resurgence trend, with an arcade full of new and classic games. The Food for Thought Café serves vegan-friendly dishes as well as carnivore pleasing burgers. All ages are welcome at the club, however, they strictly ID people buying drinks at the bar and enforce DC's curfew.

LGBTQ clubs

The Bachelor's Mill

1104 8th Street SE; tel: 202-546-5979;
www.thebachelorsmill.com

One of the oldest and largest clubs catering exclusively to the gay community, it has three fully-stocked bars, and two rooftop patios. This venue is more for gathering to kicking back and relax rather than live the bar scene. There are pool tables, big screen TVs, and a video gaming system. On weekends, there's a dance party and, more often than not, a drag show on Saturday night.

Nellie's Sports Bar

1104 U Street NW; tel: 202-332-6355;
www.nelliessportsbar.com

One of the cornerstones of the revival of the U Street corridor, this sports-lover's hangout offers burgers and other sports bar fare, big screen TVs, and as many debates about teams, owners, and other sports news as you would want to hear. A calendar of other events includes drag bingo, Movie Mondays, and karaoke nights. The Drag Brunch has a show with impersonators of Beyonce, Lady Gaga, and Diana Ross,

Crowd at the Black Cat

among others, with a large breakfast brunch; your first mimosa or Bloody Mary is included in the price.

The Fireplace

2161 P Street NW; tel: 202-293-1293; www.fireplacedc.com

A neighborhood place with a diverse crowd; the scene is older than most gay bars in the city. The bar is known for its robust drinks, which can be enjoyed in the cozy downstairs bar where a fire blazes in the winter months. The upstairs has more of a club feel with darker lighting, DJs, and dancing.

Comedy clubs

DC Improv Comedy Club

1140 Connecticut Avenue NW; tel: 202-296-7008; www.dcimprov.com

This place has been giving budding comedians their start for 25 years now. It's a clubby underground venue with a full restaurant that's busy even when there is no show. The schedule is a mix of national and regional talent. On nights when there is no comedy show, entertainment includes trivia nights, a monthly open mic night, and the occasional murder mystery evening. The improv skills and historical knowledge of local talent is tested on the clubs Time Machine Roast, when historical figures try to insult each other.

The Capitol Steps

Ronald Reagan Building and International Trade Center, 1300 Pennsylvania Avenue NW; www.capsteps.com

This legendary satirical comedy troupe was started by a group of Senate staffers. Looking for some different entertainment for the annual Christmas party, they decided to perform some parodies and skits about Congress and the White House. About half of the performers are former congressional and senate staffers. They've recorded 30 albums and regularly appear on NPR and at live venues throughout the region. Each show includes fresh material, based on a new personality or situation that is waiting to be skewered. The troupe performs every Friday and Saturday night at the Amphitheater of the Ronald Reagan Building and International Trade Center (1300 Pennsylvania Avenue NW). Tickets often sell out well in advance but can be purchased online through Ticketmaster.

Underground Comedy

1345 Connecticut Avenue NW; www.undergroundcomedydc.com

Getting great reviews as the new home for DCs comedy and improve scene, this club has an unlikely venue; in the basement of The Big Hunt, one of DC's oldest beer bars. The club space is tiny and dark, making performances intimate. There's limited seating near the stage, but most people opt to stand in the back. Mid-week, there are free shows with local talent and new professionals. On weekends, a $15 ticket gets you into the show to watch a rising star from the comedy field performing.

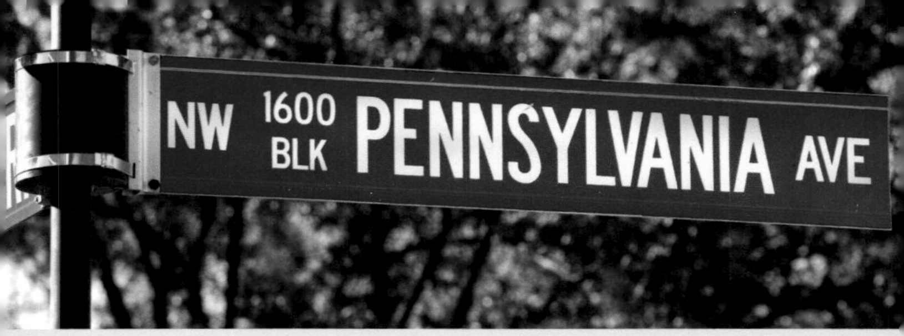

A–Z

A

Admission charges

Almost every attraction worth seeing is free of charge. The fee for most others is usually nominal. However, some of the larger museums, like the International Spy Museum and the Newseum, have higher entrance fees. Ticket prices for performances vary greatly.

Addresses

Washington is roughly diamond-shaped and is divided into four quarters. The Mall and East Capitol Street divide the city east-to-west, while North and South Capitol streets bisect the city north-to-south. Streets running north-to-south are numbered; those running east-to-west are lettered. In addition, some streets named for states run diagonally from key locations. When looking up an address, pay attention to the suffix: Massachusetts Avenue NW, or L Street SE.

Age restrictions

The legal drinking age is 21. Expect to show a photo ID at bars, restaurants, and liquor stores. You must be 21 to have an unrestricted driver's license. The age of consent for sexual activity is 16.

B

Budgeting

The money you save from free admissions is largely lost in accommodations and meal costs. Washington is one of the priciest cities in the country. A decent hotel can easily cost $200 a night. If you travel in the off-season (winter and late summer) and search for deals, you can trim the cost. Staying in Alexandria or the Maryland suburbs will definitely save money on lodging, but you have to consider the trade-off with transportation costs and time.

Average costs:
Beer: $4–6
A glass of house wine: $6–8
Cocktails: $8–15
Dining
Main course at a budget restaurant: $12–15
Moderate price: $20–30
Expensive: $40–50
Washington has dozens of food trucks, which line downtown streets at lunchtime with every cuisine on offer. The Food Truck Fiesta app shows truck locations and menus.
Hotels
Budget: $120
Moderate: $200
Expensive: $300 and up

Sledding on the US Capitol lawn

Washington has embraced Airbnb. Check for private rooms, condos, apartments, and even whole houses (www.airbnb.com).

There are several tourist cards that offer discounted admission to attractions. Tickets can provide admission to between three and five attractions from a list of 17 to 20 (www.citysightsdc.com and www.smartdestinations.com).

C

Children

Washington is child-friendly, child-tolerant, and child-hostile, depending on the venue and/or the activity. There is no lack of activities for kids, many of which are free. Those that charge admission often have discount child prices. Keep in mind that in high season, lines will be long, and temperatures will be high.

Many places do not allow strollers. They are tolerated on public transportation. A child carrier is a better option.

Check websites of hotels for family packages. Several hotels have arrangements with bonded, vetted babysitting services.

Restaurants in DC are generally not family-oriented. That said, even places beloved by the power brokers, like Old Ebbitt Grill near the White House, have a children's menu (including Mac & Cheese, hot dogs, PB & J – $9). Restaurants near major attractions are well prepared for kids.

Climate

Washington, DC has cold winters, usually with some light snow, and hot humid summers. July and August are the hottest months, with temperatures in the 90s (Fahrenheit). The summer months also have the highest rainfall due to afternoon storms. Spring and autumn temperatures are more pleasant during the day – in the 60s and 70s (Fahrenheit) – dropping slightly at night.

Clothing

Casual but considerate is the dress code. Be comfortable, but keep in mind that you are visiting seats of government, repositories of great art, and monuments to service and sacrifice. Comfortable shoes are essential. Washington is a very walkable city. For performances and fine dining, men should wear a shirt and tie.

Crime and safety

Washington has a disturbingly high crime rate. However, most crimes occur in areas that tourists do not frequent. The tourist areas are highly patrolled and safe.

Most crimes are those of opportunity. Do not flash large amounts of cash. Hang onto your purse and keep your wallet in your front pocket. Use your hotel safe. Avoid deserted areas at night. Take a taxi to a venue if you are not certain where it is.

Almost every site requires you to pass through a metal detector and have your bag inspected. Leave anything that could be interpreted as a weapon in your room.

Customs regulations

Anyone over 21 may bring 200 cigarettes, 100 cigars, or 3lbs (1.3kg) of tobacco, 1 liter of alcohol, and a maximum of $100-worth of duty-free gifts. Importing meat products, seeds, plants, or fruits is illegal, as are narcotics. Visitors entering the US may bring as much money as they wish in cash, travelers' checks, or money orders. Any amount exceeding $10,000USD must be declared upon arrival. You may take out anything you wish, but check the customs regulations of your destination country.

Disabled travelers

All public places must accommodate anyone who needs a wheelchair. Most buildings have ramps, elevators, widened doorways, and special entrances. Sidewalk curbs have cuts in them. Restrooms have stalls specifically designed for wheelchairs. Many sites offer material in Braille or large print. Some provide audio narration, usually only in English.

Disabled travelers can obtain a Metro Disability Travel Card that entitles them to discounted fares. It is valid on the Metrobus, Metrorail, MARC trains, DC Circulator bus, and Amtrak. For more information visit www.wmata.com, www.wheelchairtravel.org. The Disability Information page of www.washington.org has details of scooter and wheelchair rental.

Electricity

Standard electricity in the US is 110–120V, 60-cycle AC voltage. Laptops and many travel appliances are dual-voltage and will work, but check first. An adapter will be needed for US sockets.

Embassies

Australia: 1601 Massachusetts Avenue NW; 202-797-3000
Canada: 501 Pennsylvania Avenue NW; 202-682-1740
Ireland: 2234 Massachusetts Avenue NW; 202-462-3939
Italy: 3000 Whitehaven Street NW; 202-612-4400
Singapore: 3501 International Place, NW; 202-537-3100
United Kingdom: 3100 Massachusetts Avenue NW; 202-588-6500

Emergencies

For police or medical emergencies, dial 911 on any cell phone or land line. For non-emergencies:
DC Metro Police: 202-727-9099; US **Capitol Police**: 202-224-9806.

Cherry trees in full bloom around the Tidal Basin

Etiquette

US etiquette is generally very casual. People address each other in friendly, rather than formal, terms. Mr and Ms are used in business and formal settings if the person is a superior. Mrs is rarely heard or used. When meeting someone, a handshake is expected.

If you are invited to someone's home, a bottle of wine, a box of candy, or a small personal token is thoughtful. Flowers are less popular. It's best to avoid discussing politics, although you may be asked how things are viewed in your country. In general treat everyone with the same level of respect that you would expect to receive.

Festivals

January: Presidential Inauguration Day (the next one is scheduled for 2021); Martin Luther King, Jr's Birthday Observance

Late January-early February: Chinese New Year

Mid-March–mid-April: Cherry Blossom Festival

May: Memorial Day; Embassy Tours

June: Capital Pride Festival; DC Jazz Festival

Late June–early July: Smithsonian Folklife Festival

July: 4th of July parade, concert, and fireworks; Capital Fringe Festival

August: Fest Africa (Silver Spring)

September: Labor Day Weekend Concert; Hispanic Heritage Month

October: Marine Corps Marathon; Washington National Horse Show

November: Veterans Day Observances; FotoWeek DC

December: Lighting the National Christmas Tree; Georgetown Glow

Health

Inoculations: There are no vaccination requirements for visitors to the US.

Healthcare and insurance: Health care costs in the US are frighteningly expensive. Nationalized or government sponsored health plans from other countries rarely provide coverage for visitors to the US. It is very important that you purchase travel medical insurance.

Pharmacies and hospitals: In the case of a medical emergency, dial 911 on any phone. You can also go directly to a hospital emergency room.

Children's National Medical Center, 111 Michigan Avenue NW; tel: 202-476-5000

The George Washington University Hospital, 900 23rd Street NW; tel: 202-715-4000

Georgetown University Hospital, 3800 Reservoir Road NW; tel: 202-444-2000

Howard University Hospital, 2041 Georgia Avenue NW; tel: 202-865-6100

Washington Hospital Center, 110 Irving Street NW; tel: 855-546-1686.

The White House lit up in rainbow colors

'Immediate Care Centers' provide medical treatment on a walk-in basis for minor problems.

Metro Immediate Care: 1101 15th Street SW (tel: 202-798-0100); Farragut Medical and Travel Care: 815 Connecticut Avenue NW (tel: 202-775-8500).

Pharmacies sell over-the-counter remedies that do not need prescriptions. If you need prescription medication be sure you bring enough with you.

The largest pharmacy chain is CVS. It has several 24-hour stores, including 1275 Pennsylvania Avenue NW (tel: 202-638-4583); 6 DuPont Circle NW (tel: 202-785-1466); 1403 Wisconsin Avenue NW, Georgetown (tel: 202-337-4848).

I

Internet facilities

Free Wi-Fi is almost ubiquitous. Nearly every hotel offers free Internet. There is free coverage on the National Mall, in front of the Supreme Court, the Library of Congress, the Capitol Visitors' Center, and all public libraries. The Metro subway system is installing free Wi-Fi in all stations.

L

LGBTQ travelers

DuPont Circle and Adams Morgan are the hubs of the gay scene. The *Washington Blade* (www.washington blade.com) is the oldest LGBT newspaper in the US. *Metro Weekly* (www.metroweekly.com) and *tagg magazine* (www.taggmagazine.com) carry entertainment listings.

M

Media

Newspapers

Washington has dozens of newspapers, catering to every interest, ethnic group, political philosophy, and social cause. They are free and found at street corner kiosks. The *Washington City Paper* is a free paper that focuses on lifestyle.

The primary daily paper is *The Washington Post*. It is the capital's oldest daily paper and enjoys a respected international reputation. Its motto, 'Democracy Dies in Darkness', reflects its relationship with the Washington political establishment. The Friday 'Weekend' section has information about shows, exhibits, and special events.

The Washington Times is also published daily. Founded by Sun Myung Moon and owned by the Unification Church, it positions itself as the conservative response to what it views as the *Post*'s liberal bias. While the ownership is often viewed with skepticism, it attracts respected conservative contributors.

The *Washingtonian* (www.washingtonian.com) is a glossy monthly magazine covering local issues, news, and personalities. Their 'Best Of' issues are

Newspaper kiosks at Dupont Circle

good sources of recommendations for restaurants and shops.

Find foreign newspapers at Today's News, inside the National Press Building at 14th and F streets NW.

Radio stations

More than 50 AM and FM radio stations serve metro DC. Formats change frequently. www.radio-locator.com and www.radiolineup.com are databases of stations and their current format.
88.5 WAMU: news and public affairs; National Public Radio
90.9 WETA: classical music and public affairs; National Public Radio
103.5 WTOP: news, weather, and traffic

Television stations

Hotels have at least a basic cable package. The Weather Channel gives forecasts. Washington's television stations include outlets for ABC (WJLA), NBC (WRC), CBS (WUSA), Fox, Univision, and Public Television (WETA).

Money

Currency

The basic unit of money is the dollar ($), which is made up of 100 cents. Dollars come in denominations of $1, $5, $10, $20, $50, and $100. Each bill is the same size, shape, and color (green), so check the dollar amount on the face of the bill. The dollar itself is broken into the penny (1 cent), nickel (5 cents), dime (10 cents), and quarter (25 cents).

Changing money

Money exchanges are not commonly found and many banks are not equipped to handle currency exchanges; those that do charge a high fee. ATM machines are generally a better source for instant cash and usually charge a lower fee.
You can change money at:
Dulles Airport: Concourse Level Gate C-12, C-8; Mobile kiosk on Concourse D; Gate A-32
Reagan National Airport: Terminal C
Marshall/Baltimore-Washington International Airport: Pier C; Pier E
Union Station: Travelex Office
Treasure Trove: 1305 G Street NW

Credit cards

Credit cards are accepted almost everywhere. Check with the issuing bank as to whether it charges foreign transaction fees. You may be required to show photo ID when using a credit card.

Cash machines

ATMs (automatic teller machines) are found almost everywhere. They are the best source for immediate cash and charge a reasonable rate for currency exchange. Most of them apply a use surcharge of $1–2.50. The Allpoint ATM Network provides fee-free ATMs worldwide. CVS, Walgreens, and RiteAid Pharmacies have Allpoint ATMs. To find out if your bank or credit card is part of the program, visit www.allpointnetwork.com.

Shops in Georgetown

Travelers' checks

Many places no longer accept travelers' checks. Some hotels will still exchange checks for local currency, but may charge a high exchange rate.

The primary issuers of travelers' checks are American Express, MasterCard, Travelex, and Visa. Most use the form of a pre-paid credit or debit card. In Washington, branches of Sun Trust Bank will cash American Express travelers' checks.

Tipping and taxes

Service personnel depend on tips for a large part of their income. With a few exceptions, gratuities are not automatically added to your bill. As a general rule, 20 percent is the going rate. Porters and bellboys usually get $1 per bag. Housekeepers get $1 per day, per person or per room at hotels.

Sales and other taxes are added onto the listed price for accommodations, food, and purchases. In Washington, the general sales tax is 5.75 percent. It is 10 percent for restaurant meals, takeout food, rental cars, and alcohol purchased for off-premises consumption. The hotel room tax is 14.5 percent. There is no sales tax on groceries or prescription and over-the-counter medications.

In Maryland, the sales tax is 6 percent. There's a 9 percent alcoholic beverage tax.

Northern Virginia's sales tax is 6 percent.

Opening hours

Museums are generally open daily from 10am–5.30pm. Smaller attractions may close on Sundays.

Business hours are 9am–5pm. Stores open at 9am or 10am and stay open until 9pm. Larger supermarkets and some pharmacies are open 24hrs Banks are open 9am–2pm on weekdays. Some branches are open on Saturdays and have evening hours on Friday.

All government offices, banks, and post offices close on public holidays. Public transportation may run less frequently.

Post

The US Postal Service is an independent system that provides mail and parcel services. The basic rate for a first-class letter within the US is $0.49. A postcard is $0.34. There are standard, flat rate, and priority options for shipping parcels.

The basic rate for a postcard or letter to Europe or Australia is $1.15. Parcels are expensive. A small flat rate box is $35 and quickly goes to $100 for large boxes. You need to fill out customs forms to mail packages overseas.

You can buy postage stamps and ship packages at post offices. There is a post office in Union Station. Others downtown: 2 Massachusetts Avenue NW;

The Capitol Christmas Tree

1400 Independence Avenue NW; 1750 Pennsylvania Avenue NW. Many hotels can also mail letters and postcards.

Mail boxes are dark blue and stand about 3ft (1 meter) high. They are often on street corners. However, with security concerns, they are not as common downtown.

Public holidays

January: New Year's Day; Martin Luther King Day (3rd Monday)
February: Presidents Day (3rd Monday)
March/April: Easter Sunday
May: Memorial Day (last Monday)
July: Independence Day (July 4)
September: Labor Day (1st Monday)
October: Columbus Day
November: Thanksgiving Day (last Thursday) and following Friday
December: Christmas (25th)

Religion

Virtually every religion is represented in Washington. www.churchfinder.com and www.churchangel.com lists Christian churches by denomination. The Islamic Center of Washington is at 2551 Massachusetts Avenue NW. www.mavensearch.com lists synagogues.

Smoking

Smoking is prohibited in public places. That includes banks, stores, restaurants, theaters, sports arenas, and health care facilities. Hotels may offer the option for a smoking or non-smoking room.

T

Telephones

Dialing codes
The country code for the US and Canada is +1.
The international codes for Australia +61; Ireland +353; UK +44.
The area code for Washington is 202.

Mobile (cell) phones
Phone providers charge high roaming fees for foreign customers using their phones in the US. Call your provider and see if it offers a package for overseas travel. Another option is to buy a pre-paid calling card. Lastly, you can purchase a local pre-paid SIM card. You have the option of 'pay as you go' or 'unlimited'. Pay as You Go is similar to most European plans. Unlimited plans are similar to those in Canada, Australia, and New Zealand.

Time zones

Washington is in the Eastern Time Zone, which is either 4 or 5 hours behind Greenwich Mean Time, depending on whether Daylight Savings Time is in effect. Noon in Washington is also noon in New York City and 4pm in London from the first Sunday in November through the second Sunday in March.

The rest of the year noon in DC and New York means 5pm in London.

Toilets

Restrooms can be found at all museums and other attractions. Restaurants and stores generally limit use of their toilets to customers. There are no free-standing public toilet facilities.

Tourist information

For tourist information on Washington, DC visit the official website https://washington.org.

Tours and guides

Several companies offer cruises along the Potomac River. Boomerang Boat Tours has party cruises and a family adventure on a replica pirate ship (www.ridetheboomerang.com). Entertainment Cruises offers dinner and sightseeing cruises, as well as a water taxi with stops along the Potomac and to Alexandria. (www.entertainment cruises.com).

Transportation

Arrival

The major international airport is Washington Dulles International Airport (IAD). It is 26 miles (42km) west of Washington. Reagan National Airport (DCA) is 5 miles (8km) south of the city and is used primarily for domestic flights. Baltimore Washington International Airport (BWI) is 35 miles (56km) north of the city.

Airport shuttles: Many hotels offer free shuttle service from the hotel to the airport. Ask when you make reservations.

Commercial airport shuttle vans (www.theairportshuttle.com; www.super shuttle.com; and www.supremeairport shuttle.com) go directly to major hotels. Reservations are required. They cost between $25–70.

DCA Airport Taxi Cab (www.shuttle-wizard.com) handles reservations for several shuttle, car, and limo services at Reagan National.

Taxis

Dulles: Washington Flyer Taxicabs are the only cabs allowed to operate at Dulles Airport. Follow the signs for Ground Transportation or Taxi. Reservations are recommended (tel: 703-572-8294) Approximate fare is $80. If you prefer a reserved limo, Washington Sedan Service (www.washingtoniadtaxi.com) has a fleet of official-looking, black SUVs.

Reagan National Airport: Proceed from Baggage Claim to the curbside, where taxi lines are clearly marked. If you need wheelchair accessible cabs, please call 703-417-4333 24 in advance. If paying by credit card, please notify the taxi dispatcher. Approximate fare: $15.

Baltimore-Washington International (BWI): BWI Airport Taxi is the exclusive supplier of taxi transportation. Cabs are found curbside outside all Baggage Claim areas. If you require wheelchair accessible transportation, please call

Union Station railway platform

410-859-1100 in advance. There are manned desks near Baggage Claim at A-Pier and D-Pier. All cabs accept major credit cards. Approximate fare: $90.

Train and metro

Dulles: There is no direct Metro service from Dulles to DC. The closest station is the Wiehle-Reston East stop on the Silver Line. It's a 10-minute bus ride from Dulles to the Metro stop. Buses depart every 15–20 minutes. The bus stop is on the arrivals level at door 4. From Wiehle-Reston East, you take Metro Rail on the Silver Line into downtown DC. The rate varies depending on your final destination.

Reagan National Airport: Washington Metrorail Subway has an elevated Metrorail station connected to the concourse level of Terminals B and C. From Terminal A, use the Airport Shuttle bus. Get off at Terminal B/C. The stop is on the Blue and Yellow lines. It costs less than $6.

BWI Airport: Both regional Amtrak and commuter MARC trains connect BWI to Union Station. The Penn MARC line takes about 35 minutes. While service is frequent during the week, there are fewer trains on weekends. One way fares are $7 if purchased at ticket kiosks; $12 if purchased on the train.

Amtrak runs from the BWI\Marshall Rail Station to Union Station. A free shuttle service runs from the airport to the train station. The cost of the ticket varies between $15–45 one way. Trains depart several times an hour. Note that some trains do not allow passengers to bring checked baggage. The Amtrak website has more information and handles reservations (www.amtrak.com).

Bus

Dulles: Metrobus service between Dulles and downtown runs at least once an hour. The trip takes about an hour. It costs $7; $3.50 for seniors and those with disabilities. You will get off at either Rosslyn Metro or L'Enfant Plaza Metro.

Reagan National Airport: There is no public bus transportation to downtown DC.

BWI Airport: Metrobus service operates between Greenbelt on the Metro Green line and BWI. It takes about 30 minutes to reach the Greenbelt stop and another 30 via Metro to Union Station. The bus departs about once an hour. The bus costs $6, plus the fee for the Metro.

Highway

Interstate 95 (I-95) runs the length of the US from Maine to Canada. As it reaches Washington, a branch of it (I-495, also known as The Capital Beltway) circles the city. I-270 connects with I-495 from the northwest. I-66 connects with I-495 from the southwest.

Getting around DC

Washington is very easy to navigate and most points of interest are within a small area so walking is an easy option. However, sights are not as close as they appear on a map or when you see them down the street.

Bicycle: Despite the heavy traffic, cyclists manage quite well in the city. The Mall and Capitol Hill area are particularly good for cycling. See page 24 for bicycle rental options.

Driving: In a word, don't. DC traffic is notoriously difficult. Roads change direction or merge unexpectedly; turns zig-zag across intersecting streets; parking is hard to find and very expensive. If you do drive, remember traffic in the US is on the right side of the road.

Car rental

You need a valid driver's license from your home country and a credit card for deposit and payment. You must be at least 25 years old. Automatic transmission is the norm; you will not find a car with standard transmission. You will be offered GPS or SatNav as an option. That's a good idea, but the daily fee is high. If you have a portable system, download the US database at home.

In addition to the cost of the rental, agencies will add on various fees and taxes. This is particularly true at airport locations. Insurance offered by rental companies is expensive. See if your auto insurance or credit card covers rental cars.

If you are traveling with children, you need an approved child restraint seat.

Drunk driving is a serious offense. You can be arrested if your blood alcohol level is over 0.07 percent in Washington; 0.08 percent in Maryland and Virginia.

The major car rental firms include Enterprise, Budget, Alamo, Avis, and Hertz.

Taxis

The best places to find taxis are along the busier streets or at hotels and major attractions. Cabs have a panel on the roof that indicates if it is available. Raise your arm to flag the cab down. The minimum fare is $3.25; the mileage charge is $0.27 per eighth of a mile. Each additional passenger is $1. Drivers are prohibited from refusing transportation except in cases of disorderly behavior. You can pay in cash or by credit card. Always take the receipt as it has the name and number of the cab. If you leave something behind or want to file a complaint, you need this information.

You can download the app for DC Taxi (www.dctaxi.com). Other companies are Diamond Cab (tel: 202-387-2221); Yellow Cab (tel: 202-546-7900).

Metro subway

The DC Metro subway system is well planned and easy to navigate. Its network laces through DC and neighboring Virginia and Maryland. It can be pricey, even with a multi-day, off-peak time travel card. If you are traveling within the tourist districts, the DC Circulator bus is generally just as fast and convenient, and it goes to places the Metro does not (like Georgetown).

Bus travel

The Washington Metropolitan Area Transit Authority (www.wmata.com) also

Foggy Bottom–GWU Metro Station

operates the DC Metrobus. The base fare is $2 ($1 for seniors). Transfers between bus routes are free. However, if you are not familiar with the city, knowing which bus line to use is often hard to figure out. The website has excellent trip planning tools.

If you are staying within the tourist area the DC Circulator bus is much better value; the fare is $1 per ride. There are no free transfers between routes. The buses travel six color-coded routes that roll past all the popular sites. Buses run every ten minutes between stops. The map is very simple to follow. The Next Bus app pinpoints your location and tells you when the next bus will arrive (www.dccirculator.com).

V

Visas and passports

Immigration and visitation procedures can change rapidly depending on real and perceived threats to security.

To enter the United States, foreign visitors need a passport and many also need a visa. You may be asked to provide evidence that you intend to leave the United States after your visit is over (usually in the form of a return or onward ticket).

You may not need a visa if you are a resident of one of 27 countries that participate in the Visa Waiver Program and are planning to stay in the US for less than 90 days. Consult the nearest US embassy or consulate in your home country or check www.travel.state.gov. You must, however, log onto the Electronic System for Travel Authorization's unmemorably named site, www.cbp.gov/travel/international-visitors/esta at least 48 hours before traveling and provide personal information and travel details; either your application will be accepted or you will be told to apply for a visa. For the most current information, visit www.dhs.gov.

W

Weights and measures

The US uses the imperial system for measurement, Fahrenheit for temperature, and the mile for distance.

Women travelers

Washington is generally a safe place for women travelers, even solo ones. Assaults are rare in the popular areas. The same rules that apply for personal safety at home apply here. Stay away from deserted areas. If in doubt, take a taxi to a location or pick a different activity. Stay alert at bars and dance clubs. If you feel threatened, dial 911. That is the universal emergency number. Dispatchers will send help and, if needed, stay on the line until it arrives.

Dustin Hoffman and Robert Redford in All the President's Men

BOOKS AND FILM

The people and power of Washington make the city a natural subject for books and films. There's not a moment of the city's history that hasn't been written about, either in novels or movie scripts. Together they give insights into how the nation achieved all it has.

The following is a roster of some books and films that can add to your understanding of the city.

BOOKS

Insiders

The Residence: Inside the Private World of the White House by Kate Andrews Brewer. Former and current staffers respectfully open up about working in the world's most famous residence. No juicy gossip, but interesting stories about family life, formal functions, and witnessing critical events.

This town: Two Parties and a Funeral – plus Plenty of Valet Parking – in America's Gilded Capital by Mark Leibovich. An often funny but bitterly scathing critique of the effects that lobbyists and self-interest have on Washington.

Urban Legends and Historic Lore of Washington, D.C. by Robert Pohl. A fun book that recounts some of the stories of the city in this lively history.

The Nine: Inside the Secret World of the Supreme Court by Jeffrey Tobin. Granted rare interviews with the judges and their clerks, Tobin profiles the justices and talks about the functioning of the Court and how it has changed over the years.

Fire and Fury: Inside the Trump White House by Michael Wolff. The must-read behind-the-scenes account of Trump's first year in the White House.

Biography

Promise Me, Dad: A Year of Hope, Hardship, and Purpose by Joe Biden. A moving memoir about the year in which Biden balanced his duties as Vice President with the heart-wrenching reality of watching his son die of cancer.

Sisters First: Stories of Our Wild and Wonderful Life by Jenna Bush Hager and Barbara Pierce Bush. The daughters of one president and granddaughters of another, they grew up in the public eye and were often the subject of gossip for their high jinx. They tell stories about their most unusual and exciting childhood.

What Happened by Hilary Clinton. Clinton's memoir about her presidential bid and loss to Donald Trump.

Obama: An Intimate Portrait by Peter Souza. Souza was the official White House photographer. As such he took over 3 million photos during the Obama presidency. The book shows over 300 and includes the stories behind them, chronicling official, casual, and critical moments.

Fiction

The Beautiful Things that Heaven Bears by Dinaw Mengetsu. A lyrical, critically-acclaimed novel about an Ethiopian refugee and his struggle to adjust to life in America.

Lost in the City by Edward P. Jones. Original short stories that examine the lives of African Americans in DC.

The Night Gardener by George Pelicanos. One of a series of well-written crime novels set in and around the city.

For Kids

House Mouse, Senate Mouse by Peter Barnes. Kids learn how laws are made when the Squeaker of the House and the Mouse-jority Leader of the Senate pass a bill to establish a National Cheese.

The Worst Class Trip Ever by Dave Barry. An 8th grade class trip becomes an adventure as the kids try to protect the President from mysterious men.

MOVIES

Dramas

Seven Days in May (1964) Military leaders plot to overthrow the president because he supports a nuclear disarmament treaty and they fear a Soviet sneak attack.

Dr. Strangelove, or How I Learned to Stop Worrying and Love the Bomb (1964) Stanley Kubrick's dark comedy about an insane general who starts a nuclear war.

All the President's Men (1976) Hollywood's adaptation of the Woodward and Bernstein book about the Watergate break-in and collapse of the Nixon administration.

13 Days (2000) Gripping film version of the Cuban Missile Crisis.

Breach (2007) Closely based on true events. A tightly-written film about a new recruit to the FBI assigned to discover whether a career agent is actually a spy.

Comedies

Wag the Dog (1997) A TV producer fakes a war to boost the president's ratings.

Man of the Year (2006) A TV late-night comedian is elected president because of glitches in a computerized voting system.

Biopics

Nixon (1995) A biopic about the end of his presidency.

W (2008) Oliver Stone biopic about George W's decision to mend his free-wheeling ways and set his sights on the White House.

Jackie (2016) Natalie Portman was critically acclaimed for her portrayal of Jackie Kennedy in the weeks following her husband's assassination.

LBJ (2017) Woody Harrelson stars as the powerful senator who becomes a powerless Vice President until the Kennedy assassination.

ABOUT THIS BOOK

This *Explore Guide* has been produced by the editors of Insight Guides, whose books have set the standard for visual travel guides since 1970. With top-quality photography and authoritative recommendations, these guidebooks bring you the very best routes and itineraries in the world's most exciting destinations.

BEST ROUTES

The routes in the book provide something to suit all budgets, tastes and trip lengths. As well as covering the destination's many classic attractions, the itineraries track lesser-known sights, and there are also excursions for those who want to extend their visit outside the city. The routes embrace a range of interests, so whether you are an art fan, a gourmet, a history buff or have kids to entertain, you will find an option to suit.

We recommend reading the whole of a route before setting out. This should help you to familiarise yourself with it and enable you to plan where to stop for refreshments – options are shown in the 'Food and Drink' box at the end of each tour.

For our pick of the tours by theme, consult Recommended Routes for... (see pages 6–7).

INTRODUCTION

The routes are set in context by this introductory section, giving an overview of the destination to set the scene, plus background information on food and drink, shopping and more, while a succinct history timeline highlights the key events over the centuries.

DIRECTORY

Also supporting the routes is a Directory chapter, with a clearly organised A–Z of practical information, our pick of where to stay while you are there and select restaurant listings; these eateries complement the more low-key cafés and restaurants that feature within the routes and are intended to offer a wider choice for evening dining. Also included here are some nightlife listings and our recommendations for books and films about the destination.

ABOUT THE AUTHOR

Fran Severn collects suitcases and carry-ons the way other women collect shoes. She has written about a school for butlers in London, worked on a cattle ranch in New Mexico, ridden camels in Morocco, and gotten lost in the back streets of Jerusalem. A private pilot, she has flown across the US and Canada. She's written over 200 articles for publications as varied as *Delta Sky* and *Western Horseman*; you can follow her travels at www.severnwriter.com. She currently lives on Maryland's Eastern Shore with her husband, three dogs and two horses.

CONTACT THE EDITORS

We hope you find this Explore Guide useful, interesting and a pleasure to read. If you have any questions or feedback on the text, pictures or maps, please do let us know. If you have noticed any errors or outdated facts, or have suggestions for places to include on the routes, we would be delighted to hear from you. Please drop us an email at hello@insightguides.com. Thanks!

CREDITS

Explore Washington, DC
Editors: Rachel Lawrence and Sian Marsh
Author: Fran Severn
Head of Production: Rebeka Davies
Update Production: Apa Digital
Picture Editor: Tom Smyth
Cartography: Carte
Photo credits: Alamy 7MR, 21L, 20/21, 31, 38, 40/41, 49, 51L, 52, 54, 62/63, 64/65, 66, 69, 77, 80/81, 83, 86, 120, 121; AWL Images 28/29T; Four Seasons 95; Getty Images 4/5T, 8ML, 8/9T, 11T, 14/15, 18/19, 22, 23, 25L, 27, 32, 50/51, 53, 58, 66/67, 75L, 79L, 78/79, 82, 84, 87, 104, 105, 107; Greg Powers 99, 100; Hyatt Corporation 92; Iron Gate 103; iStock 4ML, 4MR, 4MR, 4ML, 7M, 8MC, 8ML, 20, 24, 24/25, 28ML, 28MC, 28ML, 30, 34, 36, 37L, 36/37, 39L, 42, 43, 47L, 48, 50, 56/57, 108, 110/111, 112, 113, 115, 116, 117, 118/119; Leonardo 8MR, 90ML, 90MC, 90MR, 90MR, 90MC, 90ML, 90/91T, 93, 94, 97, 101; Public domain 6ML, 26, 28MC, 85; Rey Lopez/Under a Bushel.com 18, 98; Richard Nowitz/Apa Publications 35, 38/39; Scott Suchman 8MR, 17, 102; Shutterstock 4MC, 6MC, 6BC, 7T, 7MR, 8MC, 16, 33L, 44, 45L, 46, 46/47, 56, 57L, 59, 62, 63L, 67L, 68, 70, 71L, 72, 73, 74, 74/75, 76, 78, 80, 81L, 88/89, 109; Steveturphotg 61; SuperStock 60; The Doyle Collection 96; Washington. org 1, 6TL, 10, 11B, 12, 13L, 12/13, 19L, 28MR, 28MR, 44/45, 55, 70/71, 106, 114; White House Historical Association 4MC, 32/33
Cover credits: iStock (main) Shutterstock (bottom)

Printed by CTPS – China

First Edition 2018

No part of this book may be reproduced, stored in a retrieval system or transmitted in any form or means electronic, mechanical, photocopying, recording or otherwise, without prior written permission from Apa Publications.
    Every effort has been made to provide accurate information in this publication, but changes are inevitable. The publisher cannot be responsible for any resulting loss, inconvenience or injury.

DISTRIBUTION

UK, Ireland and Europe
Apa Publications (UK) Ltd
sales@insightguides.com
United States and Canada
Ingram Publisher Services
ips@ingramcontent.com
Australia and New Zealand
Woodslane
info@woodslane.com.au
Southeast Asia
Apa Publications (Singapore) Pte
singaporeoffice@insightguides.com
Worldwide
Apa Publications (UK) Ltd
sales@insightguides.com

SPECIAL SALES, CONTENT LICENSING AND COPUBLISHING

Insight Guides can be purchased in bulk quantities at discounted prices. We can create special editions, personalised jackets and corporate imprints tailored to your needs.
sales@insightguides.com
www.insightguides.biz

INDEX

MAP LEGEND

● Start of tour

→ Tour & route direction

❶ Recommended sight

❷ Recommended
   restaurant/café

★ Place of interest

ℹ Tourist information

✈ Airport

🗿 Statue/monument

⛪ Church

✉ Main post office

🚌 Main bus station

Ⓜ Metro station

⊕ Hospital

　 Park

　 Important building

　 Pedestrian area

　 Urban area

　 Transport hub

✝✝✝✝ Cemetery

INSIGHT ⊙ GUIDES

OFF THE SHELF

Since 1970, INSIGHT GUIDES has provided a unique perspective on the world's best travel destinations by using specially commissioned photography and illuminating text written by local authors.

Whether you're planning a city break, a walking tour or the journey of a lifetime, our superb range of guidebooks and phrasebooks will inspire you to discover more about your chosen destination.

INSIGHT GUIDES

offer a unique combination of stunning photos, absorbing narrative and detailed maps, providing all the inspiration and information you need.

PHRASEBOOKS & DICTIONARIES

help users to feel at home, when away. Pocket-sized with a free app to download, they go where you do.

CITY GUIDES

pack hundreds of great photos into a smaller format with detailed practical information, so you can navigate the world's top cities with confidence.

EXPLORE GUIDES

feature easy-to-follow walks and itineraries in the world's most exciting destinations, with our choice of the best places to eat and drink along the way.

POCKET GUIDES

combine concise information on where to go and what to do in a handy compact format, ideal on the ground. Includes a full-colour, fold-out map.

EXPERIENCE GUIDES

feature offbeat perspectives and secret gems for experienced travellers, with a collection of over 100 ideas for a memorable stay in a city.

www.insightguides.com